My Secret Addiction

Teens Write About Cutting

By Youth Communication

Edited by Al Desetta

True Stories by Teens

My Secret Addiction

EXECUTIVE EDITORS
Keith Hefner and Laura Longhine

CONTRIBUTING EDITORS
Philip Kay, Nora McCarthy, Rachel Blustain, Kendra Hurley,
Katia Hetter, Alexandra Ringe, Tamar Rothenberg

LAYOUT & DESIGN
Efrain Reyes, Jr. and Jeff Faerber

COVER ART
YC Art Dept.

For reprint information, please contact Youth Communication.

ISBN 978-1-933939-78-0

Second, Expanded Edition

Printed in the United States of America

Youth Communication ®
New York, New York
www.youthcomm.org

Table of Contents

Contents

Contents

Introduction

Teens often describe cutting (generally defined as injuring yourself on purpose, by cutting or scratching enough to draw blood) as a release. People who cut usually aren't attempting to kill themselves. Rather, cutting is a way of coping. For many teens, it can temporarily relieve emotions that would otherwise be unbearable.

In *My Secret Addiction*, teens write about their experiences with cutting, as well as what has helped them face difficult feelings in more positive ways. (Note: these stories are by girls, but boys cut, too, for similar reasons.)

In "Too Much Independence," the writer cuts herself to deal with feelings of being ignored and abandoned by her mother. She manages to give up the habit when she finds affection from others, and comes to terms with her relationship with her mom.

Gia Minetta, author of "A Long Hard Climb," has been depressed all her life. Disturbed by conflicts at home, she starts abusing alcohol in 7th grade and then moves on to cutting. When she enters therapy and learns to express her emotions, she begins to emerge from her personal darkness.

Not all of the writers have found a way to stop cutting. In "Living on a Razor's Edge," P. Carr writes about being ashamed of her need to cut. But she's not able to give up the feeling of calm that it brings her. She writes, "I believe that there is help out there. I just haven't gotten to the place where I'm ready to find it."

The last five stories in this book are devoted to the subject of therapy, and how it can help teens better manage their emotions. With candor and insight, the writers discuss both positive and negative experiences with therapy to help readers understand what to expect.

All of the writers in this book would agree that therapy can help teens stop cutting and help them understand some of the deeper issues in their lives. But they have also found that not all therapists are helpful. They encourage readers to play an active role in seeking therapists who they can connect with.

A note to adult readers: Finding out that a child or teen you care about is cutting can be disturbing. It's so unsettling, in fact, that adults often focus on trying to stop the cutting, rather than trying to understand why it's happening. We hope these stories will help you remember that cutting is a symptom. It means that a teen is dealing with something too difficult to express in any other way. Pay attention, and focus your efforts on trying to understand and empathize with the teens so you can build trust. Only then can you help the teen address the underlying issues that are causing them to seek relief.

A note to teens: If you've had experience with cutting, we hope that these stories will help you feel less isolated, and inspire you to seek better solutions. Cutting can help you cope with something that feels unbearable, and it can make you feel better. But the problems or feelings you're blocking out will come back. Distracting yourself with cutting can keep you from getting the help you need to become happier and achieve your goals.

Thomas Yip

My Secret Addiction

By Christina G.

I first cut myself when I was 13. I was feeling depressed and dead inside. I noticed a box of blades lying on the kitchen shelf. I took a blade and carried it back to my room.

I closed the door, mulled it over for about a minute, and then made a small, vertical cut, about a centimeter long, to the underside of my left wrist. At first I felt nothing, as usual, and then came the pain—like a paper cut—and the feeling that a door had been opened. My heart beat really fast and I felt a rush; I felt powerful, and alive.

Two drops of bright blood appeared, darkening as they fused into one. I squeezed and scratched in order to make the cut bleed more. After about two more drops, the blood refused to come out. Then I went to lie down and soon after came down from the rush. I felt guilty about what I'd done.

But after about a week, I tried it again. Though it may seem hard to understand, it felt good to feel something after so long feeling nothing. And soon it became a regular part of my life.

A lot of the problems that finally led me to cut myself began back in elementary school. I was extremely shy and I found myself unable to go to school. At first it was the building itself I couldn't enter. Then once I was inside the building, I couldn't go into my classroom. I would become absolutely paralyzed at the entrance.

In junior high, I used to just sit in the stairwell and cry. Lots of days I'd decide to skip school completely. When I wasn't in school, most days I'd stay home and watch television, read, write and play.

For the first two years or so, that was pretty much OK. But after that, I began to hate myself—the school situation, my weight and my shyness. I began not to care about the way I dressed, or if I got dressed in the morning at all. I'd stay up all night watching television or I'd sleep half the day. I almost never went out.

I was like this until high school. All along, adults called me crazy. In elementary school, one social worker even told me I belonged in the psychiatric ward of the hospital.

My junior high principal said that if I didn't go to class I would be taken away from my house and locked up. He once shoved me up the stairs, dragged me down the hall crying, and pushed me into my classroom. He told my class that I had "psychological problems." Needless to say, I ran out of that school and never returned.

Everyone tried to take control of my life and find out what was "wrong" with me. I was sent to a therapist against my will. They tried to push me and guide me, but they only succeeded in backing me further into the corner I was in. I began to trust only myself and became even more depressed.

By the time I was 13, I found myself growing more and more

apathetic. The first therapist I ever liked had gone on leave and I got shifted to a woman who I hated almost as much as I hated myself.

It was at that time that I started cutting myself. I would think about it first and then finally decide doing it was better than not doing it. In the beginning I usually just made one cut at a time, every few days or so. But after a while I began to make more cuts.

By the time I was 14, I was doing it several times a day, and sometimes I'd even slash myself many times in hidden places, like my chest. Most of the cuts were in places where I figured no one would ever see or think that it was deliberate.

At first I felt nothing, but then came the pain—like a paper cut—and the feeling that a door had opened. I felt powerful and alive.

I could pass off cuts on my fingers for paper cuts, for example, and cuts on my arms as accidents. I'm a very private person, so I kept it hidden as best I could. (I guess there was also a little vanity, because I never cut myself too deep in places where I didn't want scars.)

But sometimes I would open my cuts up again and make them bleed more, or poke at them with a pin or needle, all to feel more pain. Other times I'd only drag the blade across my skin just to feel the coldness and a slight burn.

Pain was something real—it was a way for me to jar my feelings, good and bad, back from wherever they had gone. I could turn to the pain whenever I wanted to. There I had ultimate power.

I started to vary my arsenal. Along with boxcutter blades, I began using things like knives, pins, needles, scissors, soda can tabs, razors, screwdrivers, and broken glass. However, the boxcutter blade remained my weapon of choice.

After I cut myself, though, I'd feel guilty about what I'd done. I wondered why I had done it, and when what I was going through would end. I decided that killing myself was the answer. I didn't have any other control in my life, so death seemed a promising alternative.

I started to think a lot about ways to kill myself. I had begun to feel dead anyway. All I knew was that I didn't want to continue the way I'd been living. Trying to kill myself didn't work the first time, and I felt like such a worthless failure that I slashed myself many times.

I tried several more times over the next year and a half. After each time, I felt really bad and cut myself. Cutting had become a way to both help and punish myself. It helped me feel something again, but also became a way for me to take out my self-hatred.

I couldn't tell anyone about what I was doing. I was afraid if anyone found out they would judge me and I would get locked up. People had already called me crazy and made threats.

Anyway, I'd seen things like that happen in movies and on TV before, too. I couldn't afford to give up my freedom. I knew my family would only make me feel worse. I didn't have any friends because I'd lost them all when I stopped going to school. I couldn't tell my therapist because I knew she was required by law to report it.

On top of all that, I fiercely guarded my privacy, so throwing myself out into the spotlight and having to face probing questions was not something I was willing to do. I was alone. The only person I had was myself.

Two years ago, I was finally able to go to school again on a regular basis. It isn't easy for me to explain what changed. School officials had tried all sorts of methods to get me to go back to school. They put me in special ed., held me back a year and changed my school on me. They even tried to send a teacher to my house.

But I didn't want any of that. So I enrolled in high school and, after a week of trying, I was finally able to enter the classroom. Though it wasn't easy at first, I began to attend classes regularly.

Once I was more involved in school, I began to talk to other teens about my experiences.

Some said that I was crazy and needed "serious psychological help;" others could empathize because they'd done it too.

Last year, a friend and I were sitting in a locker bay after lunch. I was still getting used to going to school and being around my peers and was in a very blue month. My friend and I were sitting there talking and laughing, but I felt really bad. So I broke the tab off of my soda can and began scratching at my wrist with it.

He grabbed my arm and took the tab away from me, but I stood up, ripped the can open and used that instead. My scratches were swelling a little and burning. He pleaded with me to give him the can, which I did.

Pain was something real— it was a way for me to jar my feelings back from wherever they had gone.

I felt like hell afterwards, between the guilt and having done it in front of another person for the first time. I just sat on the floor, silent, wanting to cry and disappear, but unable to do either.

After that experience I decided I wanted to stop cutting myself. I began to take control of my life. I started applying myself completely in school and doing well. I also stopped going to the therapist I didn't like. I made many friends, and started going out and doing more things. I began to say what I wanted and to do what I wanted. I began to get things for myself.

Once I started experiencing life and improving it, cutting myself became more and more of a symbol of a loss of control. It had lost its importance and meaning. I no longer needed to do that because I was no longer stuck in a rut.

Because people weren't pushing me anymore I had freedom to expand on my own. Probably most important, I didn't feel like the walking dead any longer. I stopped cutting myself and eventually stopped feeling suicidal.

Thee were times when I was tempted to do it again, like when I felt bad after my boyfriend broke up with me. But I didn't do it because I could be OK without hurting myself.

I had already come through a ton of stuff and the end of that relationship was actually one of the things that taught me that I wasn't a weak person, and that I was capable of doing anything and being happy.

It's been about a year and a half since the last time I cut myself. There was no magic involved in stopping, it just took time. When I got over my inability to go to school, many doors opened. I think that the rest all happened from there.

I don't regret what I've done. I think that it was something I needed to do, at the time. My life got worse because too many people thought they knew what was best for me, but the opposite was true. It wasn't until everyone really backed off and gave me my space that I was able to finally figure things out for myself and fix my life.

These days I am truly happy for the first time. Like everyone else, I have my highs and lows, but they don't affect me like they used to. Now, I love to have new experiences.

This spring, a friend asked me what there is to live for. It was nearing the end of the school year and he was jaded by the large amount of work to do. I told him there is a lot to live for.

"This from the formerly suicidal," I said. We laughed and continued walking.

The author was 17 when she wrote this story.

Kenly Dillard

Cutting Myself Seemed Like an Escape

By Christine M.

I usually don't remember when I cut myself. I sometimes don't know what I've done until I "come to" with my arm beating like a second heart and burning hot, fresh scars, and a sagging feeling in my chest, as if a huge weight has been lifted. Then, after the initial relief, I feel ashamed at what I've done, and terrified at how others would feel if they knew.

For years I couldn't understand why I was cutting myself and blacking out while I did it. All I knew was that my secret habit had become completely out of control. But after going into foster care and finding people who really care about me, I've begun to understand it better.

Getting a proper diagnosis of my problem, and a good therapist to help me work through it and sort out my past, has made things easier. I've realized that because of all the abuse I went through, and because I was constantly told that my feelings didn't count, cutting became one of the few ways I felt comfortable expressing and escaping all the pain I hold inside.

I can't remember ever feeling attached to my body. My skin has never felt like my own. I was sexually abused by my father and constantly hit by my mother. To survive the abuse, I believed it was happening just to my body, but not to me.

I was numb back then. Not feeling my own emotions was the only way I knew how to handle all that was going on. Instead, everything I did or felt was tied into other people's moods, especially my mother's. If by some grace of God she was in a good mood, I was relaxed and laughed easier, smiled brighter, but never forgot that any moment the tide could change. That hug could turn into a slap. Words of encouragement could soon be followed by bitter, acidic remarks. "You're doing so well in school, Chrissy! Let's see how long it takes before you screw it up."

The few times I did show any emotion, my mom would get mad. "What have you got to cry for? You have it easy! I'm the one who has to go to work every day to keep a roof over your head and food on the table!" So I kept it to myself, and did my best not to feel anger, or much of anything.

That changed when one day I saw a knife lying on the kitchen counter. "What the hell," I thought. She was already kicking my ass daily by that point, and my father was molesting me. The pain would be nothing new.

Once I felt the pressure of that cool blade against my skin, I knew this was different, very different. This was my pain and I could control it. I could make it start and I could make it stop. I didn't exactly feel better when I cut, but it let me feel something other than that horrible emptiness, that nothing I felt inside. It let me feel alive.

Soon cutting became my secret escape. My pent-up frustrations, fears, and the relentless hatred I felt toward myself seemed to disappear, at least for the moment. I was a pressure cooker waiting to explode, and cutting gave me temporary release. My bleeding arms were my form of tears.

By the time I entered the San Diego foster care system at age 14, cutting no longer gave me a sense of control. It had become out of control.

Living in a group home with six other females was jarring to me. I don't remember much from living there, just snippets, but I clearly remember the times right before I cut. Something bad would be happening that I couldn't stand: staff screaming at residents, calling them awful names for talking on the phone to guys; residents beating each other up over TV privileges; me usually sitting quietly, trying not to be noticed. But inevitably, someone always noticed. "You see Chrissy isn't talking to any boys!" It made me feel as though they were about to hit me. I would start to feel like the sides of my skull were being pressed together and I would sink inside myself. Then suddenly I would find myself in the bathroom, cutting, with staff banging on the door.

I knew this was different, very different. This was my pain and I could control it.

I could never remember how I got to the bathroom. Years later, a therapist explained that I have a mental disorder that allows me to "dissociate"—to mentally separate myself from my body when I feel too much pain. It was the way I'd managed to survive all the abuse I'd been through as a child—my mind would just go to another place. But in that first group home, all I knew was that I no longer knew how to stop cutting.

I was soon transferred to a foster home because my social worker thought a one-on-one relationship might calm me down, and at first that's what happened. I quickly noticed something strange in Ellen's house. She used words instead of fists, kind and gentle words that cared about my feelings and how I would react. I noticed that with her I laughed a lot more. I felt less jumpy and more at ease, and even a hint of something I had never really allowed myself to feel before…happiness.

I started to call Ellen "Mom," though she was the opposite of my real mother. She showed me how to cook, and wanted to know about my life. She never made me feel like I was taking up air by being alive. For the first time I felt cared for.

*E*ven though I had never told Ellen about my blackouts and inability to remember things, I somehow felt that she knew and wasn't upset about it. She seemed to realize that if she reacted calmly to me, I was less likely to become upset.

During this time I started cutting less. I could go weeks without "waking up" in the bathroom with cuts on my arm. Things were finally starting to mellow out inside my head, and I felt truly happy. But soon, things started to change back, mostly because of her boyfriend Steve.

In the beginning Steve was cool. He taught me about football and drove me and my foster sisters to the mall. But after a couple of months, he started to come into my room late at night. I was terrified.

At first, I didn't tell Ellen about it. I thought I could handle it, and I did, but at a price. I started finding burns on my legs and thin cuts close to the veins on my ankles. Usually when I cut I seemed to instinctively avoid my veins. But this was new. This felt life-threatening. It scared the hell out of me.

I also started blanking out more. Days went by without me noticing. Once I "woke up" and a whole month had passed without me remembering how I spent it. I was frightened.

After about four months I couldn't hide the cutting and blackouts anymore. I was hospitalized. I was sure Ellen would leave me, or become distant and cold when she found out about the cutting. Instead she was concerned, an emotion I never thought people could have for me. Annoyed, I could deal with. Disappointed, I knew how to handle very well. This was different. I almost couldn't handle it—I worried that if I hadn't disappointed her already, I would soon enough. Her caring made me scared and suspicious. I was determined to make her leave me.

I started to cut more, like I was saying to her, "Don't care about me, it'll only hurt you in the long run." But she never gave up. When I cut, she cleaned the wound and sat with me through the night. When I screamed and threw things across the room, trying to piss her off, she would bear hug me until I calmed down and we could talk. It was like she knew my defenses and was determined to break through them.

After the hospitalization, she set me up with the school psychologist, Dr. Eimers. He was the best school counselor I have ever met. He actually wanted to talk to me. Not just superficial stuff, like how was your day, but real stuff I desperately wanted someone to ask.

I tried to explain to him about losing time, and how I felt like I was going crazy. We also talked about my cutting. We tried to find other activities that gave me a feeling of control, since that was partly why I first started cutting. I loved being at school, because I could forget all about my problems. But what brought me the most joy was swimming, so he suggested that I join the swim team. Being underwater made me feel like I was in another world. There was only the sound of my heart and my thoughts.

It's really hard to stop doing something that, for almost half my life, was my way of coping.

But swimming wasn't enough. One day I was in the locker room at school getting ready for swim practice and I got a severe headache. The pain was so bad it brought tears to my eyes. I blinked and the next thing I knew I was in Dr. Eimer's office. He was asking if I wanted to talk about it. "Talk about what?" I asked. He looked at me kind of funny and said, "About why you started breaking the mirrors in the girls' locker room." I was horrified. I had no idea what he was talking about. To buy some time I asked if I could see the school nurse because I had a headache.

As I was waiting for the nurse, I started having flashbacks of abuse. They were running through my head so fast that I couldn't tell what was remembered and what was happening at the moment. I found myself in the bathroom with a bottle of peroxide, thought what the hell, locked the door, and swallowed the entire bottle. Then I sat back down in Dr. Eimer's office and waited to die.

I ended up in the hospital. Shortly after that I was sent to Penny Lane, a residential treatment center in San Diego, and that's when things started to really get better for me.

I would've never guessed walking into those red double doors that Penny Lane would have a good effect on me. At first it felt like hell: Fifty-two females with just three showers. Girls screaming up and down the halls. No privacy. I saw someone being restrained my first day there. Staff had her face on the tile floor, their knees pressing into her back.

I continued to blackout and to cut while I was there. But the amazing thing was that after "waking up" up in the hospital for the first time, they didn't send me somewhere new. Penny Lane took me back every time.

As much as I hated Penny Lane, it made me glad to realize they weren't going to throw me away like so many group homes and facilities had before. They didn't ridicule me or call me names about my cutting. They tried to understand why I did it, even though I didn't really know myself. And that made all the difference.

One staff, Chris, helped the most. He was one of the first men to ever care about me in a non-abusive way. He was new, and during his first week he had to watch me on a one-on-one suicide watch. I usually ignored the person assigned to watch me, but he wanted to talk. He asked about the books I read, the movies I liked, the music I listened to. It was the best thing anyone could have done for me. I was so wrapped up in my inner hell, I had forgotten life. He helped bring me back.

I grew to love him like a brother. Chris knew about the cutting and the way I lost time, but he never made me feel ashamed. Instead he said, "You must be in so much pain inside to do this to yourself." I was floored. No one had ever, ever, said that. I started to cry. It was as if a flood had been released inside my soul, and I couldn't stop it. No one else seemed to have recognized just what the cutting meant, not even me.

That was a major turning point for me. After that, when I started to get those headaches that usually ended up with me in the bathroom, I tried everything in my power to stay conscious and not cut, though a lot of times I still couldn't stop it. And I began to talk more. Mostly through poetry at first, pouring out whatever I was feeling, and that helped.

I did still cut when the pressure inside me was too much, but I also started to let in people I knew cared about me. I even got a mentor, who I remain close to now, six years later. Pamela has stuck by me through all the BS I put her through, and never stopped loving me.

Two years ago, when I emancipated from foster care, I moved from California to New York. I didn't realize how hard it would be and how alone I would feel. I found a whole new set of problems to handle in New York, but this time there was no Pamela or Chris to help me. I began to cut more.

Luckily Covenant House, where I ended up living, required that I go to therapy. I was diagnosed as having Dissociative Identity Disorder (D.I.D.). A therapist explained to me that because I was repeatedly faced with overwhelming abuse in my childhood, and since I had no physical escape or any other way of getting help, I "went away" in my head, although I had no awareness of this.

When I first discovered that I have D.I.D., I was more relieved than scared. It made sense out of so much in my life: the feelings that this wasn't my body, the constant blackouts, the lack of a real memory before the age of 12. Knowing what I had meant I could work on getting better.

I soon found a therapist who specialized in D.I.D. She helped me realize that the reason I never knew when I was going to cut myself was because I dissociate from what is going on, it's like another part of me takes over. She also said that instead of blaming me for cutting, we should try to understand why I do it.

I started to understand that I really do have feelings, many feelings. As a child, I felt so much shame, anger and pain about the abuse I endured that I didn't know how to express it, and no one helped me talk about it. So I tried to bury those feelings, but also to communicate them through hurting myself.

Now, with the help of my therapist, I'm trying to find other things I can do when I feel overwhelmed, like scribbling red all over a paper to represent blood and anger. Writing and talking also help a lot. So does staying in touch with the people who care about me.

The relief cutting used to bring me is now more short-lived, and cutting no longer helps me cope like it used to.

Still, it's hard, really hard, to stop doing something that, for almost half my life, was my way of coping. I am still a small child when it comes to handling overwhelming emotions. I can't always remind myself that those emotions will pass. And it's always easier to reach for a razor than to confront the feeling behind the impulse. But I'm getting better at stopping that from happening.

More and more I'm realizing that I am no longer a child whose voice goes unheard. I'm a woman with the capacity to love and learn, to have my words count for something. Perhaps one day, the way I thought about myself and the world when I was an insecure and abandoned girl will fade away, leaving only the woman I'm striving to become. Until that happens, I hope that one day I will no longer harm this body, a concept that is somewhat frightening to me, but something I want very much.

Christine wrote this story when she was 22.

Ana Jakimiuk-Chu

When Pain Seems a Relief

By Anonymous

When I felt so lonely I could have died, I used to cut myself. I didn't want to actually kill myself—I wanted to replace my emotional pain with the physical, and cutting worked for me.

My problems began when my father and I started growing apart. When I was little, we were almost inseparable. He bought me lots of gifts and we were really affectionate. Although I was sometimes intimidated by his quick anger, I was very much in love with him.

Though my father and I were close, he wasn't at home much. He'd go out on a Friday night and wouldn't come back until the next day. We often wouldn't know where he was. My parents fought a lot over this.

My father's absences and my parents' tension began to make me depressed. When I was small, I laughed easily and often, but when I was 10 and 11, I was sad more than I was happy. I felt that I wasn't getting any attention, and I started acting out so my parents would respond to me. The first thing I did, when I was 12, was try to run away.

Instead of going home from school, I took a different route that led away from my house. I didn't get far because a teacher spotted me and sent me home. My parents were upset. They asked why I tried to leave, but I just shrugged my shoulders. I didn't know how to tell them that they were making my house a place I didn't want to be.

My attempt to run away strained my relationship with my father. Mom told me he didn't sleep for days afterward. He began to say that I didn't like him and that he favored my little sister over me. By the time I turned 14, I felt like second best.

When I cut, it was from frustration, anger, hurt, and loneliness all mixed into one.

Maybe I was looking for someone to replace my father when, a few months before my 15th birthday, I met a new boy on the block. John (not his real name) was 18. Though I didn't realize it at the time, I was physically attracted to him because he reminded me of my father. He was a short, bow-legged Jamaican with a lopsided grin, deep dimples, and the roundest butt I'd ever seen on a boy.

My sister and I weren't allowed to date until we were 18. It was my mother's rule, though neither she nor my father told us how they'd punish us if we went out with boys.

I hadn't thought about dating until then, but I wanted to be with John. I broke my parents' rule and soon gave him my virginity. I didn't regret it. The relationship made me feel independent. I was sneaking out of the house and making late night phone calls.

Though I was afraid I might get in trouble, I didn't really think much about it because I was living for the moment. I didn't love John, but he was a great listener and friend.

A few weeks after I started dating John, my grandfather passed away. We visited my grandfather seven or eight times a year, and my mother talked to him on the phone every Friday. Though we didn't see him as much as we'd have liked, the love was there.

The night we found out that my grandfather died, my father wasn't around. When he made it home the next afternoon, my sister and I told him what happened. He looked stunned. Then he walked away. I wanted his embrace and words of comfort, but they never came.

My mother was in shock over her father's death. For days she would go without sleep. She scared me with her constant comments about how she didn't want to live anymore. What could I do to soothe my mother's pain?

The time when I felt I needed my father the most—when my mother was consumed by sorrow—he wasn't there. He left me to deal with my grandfather's death by myself. He never once asked if I was OK or if I needed to talk about it.

After the funeral, my boyfriend was the only one who comforted me; my mother was too upset. The hole in my heart—where I used to feel my father's love—was getting bigger.

Then, a few weeks after my grandfather's funeral, my parents found out about John. One Sunday, I was supposed to meet my family at my aunt's house. Instead of going straight there, I decided to hang out with John first.

Before I knew it, two hours had passed. When I finally got to my aunt's house, my cousin (who knew about John) pulled me aside and told me that my mother was worried: "I said you were with a friend." Another cousin told me that my father just left—he'd been there looking for me. That's when I got scared.

When we were ready to leave, my mother said, "You and I are gonna have to have a talk."

A t home, my father was already in bed. My mother took me into the bathroom and closed the door. "I want to ask you a question, and I want you to be honest with me. Do you have a boyfriend?"

I sighed. After a long minute of silence, I said, "Yes."

She looked at me with such intense anger that I thought she would hit me. "What did I tell you about not dating until you're 18?" she demanded.

She got it out of me that we had been together that day and that he was 18. When she asked me if we were having sex, I lied and said no.

"You always talk to me about everything—why couldn't you tell me this?" she said with hurt in her voice.

I couldn't answer.

"Now I want you to go tell your father," she said.

I thought that my mother would let the matter stay between us. She knew about my father's temper. "No," I whined. "Please don't, Mommy."

She didn't relent.

I went into the bedroom. My father was asleep. I wrung my hands and called his name. His eyes opened. "What is it?"

I paused and sighed. Then my mother walked into the room. "Your daughter has something to tell you," she announced with disgust before leaving us alone.

He frowned and told me to come to him. I walked over to the edge of his bed and knelt on the floor.

"Where were you tonight?" he asked.

I looked away from his sleep-reddened eyes and said in a low voice, "With a boy."

He started questioning me. I told him little by little about John, getting more and more scared.

"Did you have sex with him?" he asked. He gave me a hard stare, as if he were willing me to tell him the truth.

"Yes," I said in a low voice.

He glared at me and said nothing. After what felt like 10 minutes of silence, he told me flatly, "Get out of my face."

My body froze up. I thought he was going to slap me, but when he didn't, I became more afraid. It meant that he was too angry even to put his hands on me.

But at that moment I wish he had just slapped me instead. The fact that he kept his anger in made me wonder what would happen to me tomorrow, and the days after.

He didn't speak to me for about two weeks. Then one afternoon, he called me to have a talk. So he said. It wasn't a talk at all. He just hurled names at me, names that should never be said from father to daughter. They were names I'd expect to hear from a stranger on the street, not from any kind of father.

I thought that if I didn't cut, I'd hurt someone I loved instead.

When I'd been with John, I wasn't ashamed of having sex. To me it was fun, a decision I'd made for myself, a learning experience.

But I did feel ashamed when my father said those words to me. I felt dirty and guilty. I was upset because through it all, none of the names he called me was "daughter." His tone and the look on his face made me feel worthless, as if he could just disown me that very moment. I felt completely alone.

Determined to erase those horrible names from my mind, I took a razor blade from the kitchen, went into my bedroom and began slicing into my arm until I couldn't cry anymore, until I couldn't take the pain anymore, until I felt clean again.

I honestly don't remember why I used a razor that night. But as soon as I made the first cut, I loved the feeling when the blood seeped out and the cold air rushed onto the open wound and the pain was so fresh. I wanted that feeling over and over again, until the pain was too much to bear.

I remember thinking that I wanted to die, that no one loved or cared about me, and that maybe if I died, they'd feel guilty. I wanted everyone else to be in pain, too. Pills or anything else might've been too quick. If I died, I wanted to suffer first.

That same night I broke up with John. Now that my parents knew about us, I wouldn't be able to sneak out. And if I continued to see him, my mother would press statutory rape charges. I'd liked John's emotional support and the physical attention, but I wasn't heartbroken by losing him. I was more heartbroken about my parents.

Counseling helped lift my depression a bit, because I now had someone who would listen to me.

For the next few months, when I was alone in my bedroom, I continued cutting my wrist—only my right wrist because I'm left-handed—not even caring if someone noticed the open wounds.

After letting my parents down by having sex, it was almost as if I had to punish myself. When I cut, it was from frustration, anger, hurt and loneliness all mixed into one, boiling over and causing me to break.

I wasn't afraid of piercing a vein. I felt that if I did, it was just meant to happen. The only thing I was afraid of was not cutting; I thought that if I didn't cut, I'd hurt someone I loved instead. That was the scariest part.

Then my mom saw my wrist for the first time. She was by the stove when I was opening a cabinet. She asked, "What happened?" and my heart started beating fast.

I shrugged and mumbled, "I don't know."

She grabbed my hand and stretched out my arm and repeated, "What happened?"

I mumbled, "I cut my wrist."

She looked at me hard, and I could see the anger in her eyes. She took me straight to my father and showed him my arm. He, too, asked me what happened and gave me the same response—anger.

They removed sharp objects from my reach, and a couple of days later they sat me down for a long discussion. I told them about all the things I'd been feeling over the previous few years, about problems in my life I'd felt unable to talk to them about.

I told them how their constant fighting had made me feel alone. I told them that I felt I was partly to blame. Once I said that, they assured me that I had nothing to do with their differences.

They said they'd noticed a change in me. They'd known me as a happy child, and they saw that I'd stopped hanging out with friends, I stayed in my room with the door closed, and I looked sad.

My mother said that the only thing she could do was get me help. My father was silent, but I could tell by his facial expression and body language that he was uncomfortable with what I was revealing.

After that, I went to therapy every week for an hour. Counseling helped lift my depression a bit, because I now had someone who would listen to me.

Since my counselor felt that my depression and anger mostly stemmed from my father, she suggested that he sit in for a few sessions so we could talk through my problems. He came once. He never came back because he felt I was blaming everything on him. That made our interactions at home even more tense.

My mother, though, sat in on almost all of my therapy sessions. Sometimes I was too uncomfortable to talk in front of her, but counseling did make us closer. Because of the way we talked in therapy, she no longer approaches me with anger if she has a problem with me. Counseling also helped me stop blaming myself for my parents' relationship troubles.

But the fact that my parents were still hurting each other made me feel sad. Therapy didn't make that go away. And because the conflict between my father and me was so intense, I still felt worthless and filthy. I continued to cut.

When I felt depressed, it was really hard to resist cutting. I substituted the physical pain for the emotional. As crazy as this sounds, I felt a little happier after I cut. I got high. Then usually

I'd fall right to sleep.

In the morning I'd wake up, and the burning feeling in my arm would make me remember why I had to cut. My erratic emotions would return.

During counseling, I did stop cutting for a short while, but then my wrists began to itch. It was as if I had to do it, and I went back to cutting.

In truth, I really didn't want to be helped. I wanted to be stuck where I was. I was too far gone into depression. I couldn't see past the next day. I felt that the sadness would take over my whole body and swallow me and I'd die.

My counselor suggested other ways I could take out my frustrations. Some of her advice didn't help, like "Chew some gum." She also advised me to think about anything other than how I was feeling. But my emotions were so overwhelming that positive thoughts were too hard to conjure.

Some of her other ideas were more helpful. She knew I loved writing, so she told me to use pen and paper to release my feelings. I also enjoy music, so I'd sit in my room with the door locked and the sound down low.

Even so, I found myself actually needing to feel the physical pain, my only true relief. Writing and playing music didn't lift my emotional pain all the way like a razor did.

"Find someone to talk to," my counselor told me. Listening to that advice was the hardest of all. It had always been difficult for me to share my feelings, but now it felt like the people in my house were against me.

My sister was too young to understand. My father avoided me altogether. We kept it civil, only saying, "Good morning," "Good afternoon" and "Good night." I didn't hate my father, but I really didn't like him, either.

My mother and I were starting to have a close relationship again, but I didn't want to be a bother to her. She and my father were finally splitting up, and I felt selfish that my ordeal was happening at a time when she needed my support and I couldn't give it to her.

I began to see stress taking a physical toll on her. She was losing hair, and lines were becoming a part of her once-smooth skin.

Then, one morning when my father and I ended up in the bathroom at the same time, he noticed my arm. I rarely made an effort to cover up my wrists, but this time they were right in his face.

He said, "You're really sick, you know that?"

I felt a big pang in my chest, but I only rolled my eyes at him and kept on brushing my teeth. He told my mother and she started screaming about sending me to a mental hospital.

I knew my mother was reacting out of frustration with how I was hurting myself. But I also knew she just didn't get it. She didn't understand why I still had to cut.

Immediately my mother told my therapist that I was cutting, and my therapist told her to take me to a psychiatrist in case I needed antidepressants.

The psychiatrist didn't put me on medication, but he did diagnose me with a form of depression. And he gave me a warning: "If you don't want to end up in a straitjacket, you better stop hurting yourself."

I pictured myself sitting in a white padded room with my arms in a straitjacket to prevent me from cutting. I didn't want to be put away in a mental hospital. I have a big fear of being alone, of feeling like I have no one in the world to turn to. I feel as if I need to have support and someone to talk to always.

Loneliness is one of the feelings that makes me cut. Since I couldn't let myself be sent to a mental hospital, I had to get better, for my sake.

It hasn't been easy, but I've grown in spirit since I first started cutting three years ago. I'm 17 now and I haven't cut myself in six months.

The main reason is that a few months ago, my mother, my sister, and I left my father. Now home is just the three of us, and it feels OK to be myself.

Since we moved away, my father and I have had less tension and fewer things to argue about. We've had some nice moments. I know he loves me and I do love him. But the trust isn't there—I find it hard to speak with him about anything.

I really want a father-daughter relationship where I can talk to him as a friend and ask for advice. I hope we can make that happen. But I worry that he still has the ability to make me feel worthless, filthy and alone.

My mother wants more for me than depression and cutting. She envisions me as a happy woman, with the career as a writer that I've always dreamed of. I share her hopes.

Although my life has gotten so much better since I moved, I'm terrified that someday I'll feel sad again.

But I'm not scared of going back to cutting. In my mind cutting isn't wrong; it's a release, a relief. It helps when loneliness comes, when depression sets in, and when I feel ashamed of myself. It's helped me get through.

The thing that's wrong with cutting is that my therapist and my parents believe it's not mentally healthy. I don't want them or anyone else to send me away to a mental hospital.

So I'm trying to work through my emotions better. One thing I'm trying to do is let go of my anger. I tend to hold onto things, especially hurtful memories.

I'm also learning, slowly, to rely on myself for support. And I am still trying to find other ways to keep myself from cutting.

The author was in high school when she wrote this story.
She later graduated and went to college at SUNY Purchase.

Too Much Independence

By Anonymous

My mom gave birth to me one month after her 16th birthday. She was living with her parents in the Midwest, and she had to give up her childhood very suddenly. We lived with my grandma while my mother finished high school. Then we moved to New Jersey, where she went to college.

My mom wanted me to be independent, so she always treated me like an adult. I was only 3 years old when she started making me order for myself at restaurants. I felt shy and helpless, and I wanted her to just do it for me.

By the time I was 7, we'd moved to Seattle for my mother's job as a writer. She took me to school the first week so I could get used to the bus route. After that, I had to walk to the corner of

(Names and some identifying details have been changed in this story.)

my block by myself and wait for the bus. After school, I'd go to the corner store to buy snacks by myself. I never felt scared going places alone, but I sometimes felt bored and lonely because I had no one to keep me company.

For a long time, I felt more grown up than my friends. Their moms would baby them and hold their hands in the street. I had one 8-year-old friend whose mother still had her drinking from a bottle. I remember laughing about it with my mom because I thought my friend was so immature.

When I was 13, we moved to New York City. That's where my mom had always wanted to live, because she thought writers were supposed to live in New York. We had no furniture at first and all of our household belongings were locked away in some storage warehouse for six months (we didn't have enough money to get them out).

I wasn't adapting well to my new school. I didn't know anyone, and everyone was loud and unfriendly. I felt out of place and shy in New York. I was desperate to be back in Seattle, where I felt comfortable and accepted.

My mom was usually out with her friends or holed up in her bedroom working on one of her writing assignments. That wasn't unusual, but now that I was having a hard time, I felt abandoned.

I got into a bad relationship, some girls in my school didn't like me because of boy drama, my friends weren't loyal and my grades were dropping. On top of all that, my mom and I were constantly bumping heads at home. I felt alone and depressed, and I needed her to help me.

Every time my mom and I encountered each other, we'd get into a heated argument, slam doors and both go to bed crying. Our fights were about stupid and unimportant things. One time we got into a fight because my mom hadn't done the laundry, so I didn't have any clean clothes to wear to school the next day.

We argued for what seemed like hours, and then I screamed, "You're such a bad mother!"

Her eyes watered and she left the room. Now that I'm older, I feel horrible that I said that to her. I realize she really didn't have time to do laundry. But I don't think that was what we were fighting about anyway. She was stressed from work, and I was stressed from school. I guess we took our stress out on each other.

But I was also angry because I needed her to be a more "normal" mother. I wanted my mother's affection but I also wanted her to be strict and set boundaries with me—like giving me a curfew and getting on my back about homework. I wanted her to pay more attention to me, even if it was just her asking how my day went. All of that would have shown me that she cared about me.

I wanted so badly for someone to notice what I was going through that I began cutting myself at the end of 8th grade.

I wanted her to be like my best friend Janeen's mother, who was always there for her kids. She cooked and cleaned the house, and she asked how their day went. She even had a specific "homework" time. And every time I went over to Janeen's house, her mom would come up with fun games to play, rent us movies and make a special sleepover casserole.

My mom just wasn't that nurturing type of person. She was better at being a sister than a mother. But if she had taken time out of her busy life to comfort me, things might have been a little easier for me.

I wanted so badly for someone to notice what I was going through and to pull me out of my darkness that I began cutting myself at the end of 8th grade. One day my mom saw the cuts and asked me about them, but she didn't try to stop me. I think she knew that I was doing it for attention, so she decided to ignore me.

But some of my teachers noticed, too. "What happened to your arm?" a teacher asked me one day.

"My cat scratched me," I said.

But I knew she didn't buy it. Two of my other teachers noticed also, and all three of them set up a conference after school in a classroom with my mother and me to see if anything could be resolved. I don't remember exactly what happened in that room, but I remember feeling cornered, embarrassed and vulnerable.

My mom expressed concern about me during the meeting, but she told me afterward that only I could stop cutting myself. She never asked me to stop. Her only message was for me to take care of myself. Once again, she demanded that I be independent.

My mother and I left school that night without resolving anything, and I kept cutting myself. But during the summer after 8th grade, I visited my grandma and she saw the marks on my arm. She burst into tears and told me that she'd had a dream about me cutting myself one night, but she hadn't thought it could be true.

My grandma was heartbroken and I felt horrible that I'd made her feel that way. She was in hysterics as she begged me to stop and to never do it again. I love her so much, and her reaction had a big impact on me not cutting so much, and eventually stopping. I can see now that my grandma was the mother figure I needed to act like the adult, take charge and convince me to stop.

"What happened to your arm?" a teacher asked me one day. "My cat scratched me," I said.

The next year I met my boyfriend, David, and he helped me deal with my feelings about my mom. When my mother and I argued, I'd call him and he'd talk to me for hours until I felt better.

I remember at my worst point of cutting, my entire left arm from the top part of my wrist all the way up to my shoulder was covered in cuts. By the middle of 9th grade, I only had a few cuts on my forearm. I had come a long way.

It took David to convince me to stop cutting completely. He gave me an ultimatum one night over the phone. He said, "Baby, if you ever cut yourself again, I'll break up with you."

The problem all along was that I felt alone and thought no

one really cared. I think my grandmother and David showed me the love I needed. Once they showed me that I meant something to them, I stopped cutting.

I never talked about this episode with my mother, because she always taught me that I could only rely on myself. But my experience showed me that she was wrong. I can't always do everything for myself. There are moments in life when I need to know I'm worth something to someone else.

Looking back, I understand that my mom was a struggling young single mother going through a lot. She was extremely busy working on her writing just to pay the bills and provide us with food. She didn't have the time, energy or emotional strength to deal with helping me when she could barely help herself.

But at the time I felt like she was being self-centered and neglectful, and maybe she was. When I was going through the pain of becoming a teenager and adapting to a new city, I needed my mother to reach out to me and try to understand me. Even if she thought I was cutting myself for attention, she should have given me what I needed. At the time I thought that she must not care about me.

I wish that she had just taken me aside for a few minutes, held me by my shoulders, looked into my eyes and told me that she loved me and was there for me. I know it sounds so simple, but sometimes the answer to a complicated situation is just as simple as that.

I am grateful for the things my mom did teach me. Because of her, I am a more independent person. Because of her, I know what it's like to live in a suburban white neighborhood and a big city with millions of people from different backgrounds and cultures.

Just by exposing me to different environments, my mom helped me form my own opinions about different lifestyles. When I grow up, I'll choose where I want to live and how I want to lead my own life.

But that doesn't mean I'm going to raise my kids the way she raised me. When my boyfriend and I have kids of our own someday—probably a few years after we graduate from college and can provide them with a good life—we plan to do things differently.

We're going to incorporate a little of the traditional parenting style that David's mother gave him, using some Catholic traditions, supervision, boundaries and rules, with a little bit of the independence that my mother used with me. I think that it's important for children to be children while they're young, and to provide them with some kind of structure before gradually easing them into independence.

I want my children to feel like they can come to me for anything, that I will be there for them, and that they can trust me. Yeah, independence is important. But no one can be 100% independent all the time. Every now and again it's necessary for kids and adults to have someone to lean on. I know that for a fact.

The author was 17 when she wrote this story.

Asaiah Ajibabi

Drifting Away

By T. Mahdi

My mental illness is part of me. I look at those seven words and I say, "Oh God, how the hell am I going to accept that?"

I go back to last year when it all began. I was 18 and my sister and I had just moved in with our new foster mom, my love, Yolonda.

I realized that I had a problem when I sat in the dark for hours, talked to myself, dissociated (separated from my body) and cut myself. A therapist told me that I was suffering from depersonalization and depression.

Depersonalization means that you can take yourself out of a situation or reality and put yourself, mentally, in a safe place. It sounded like a long word for crazy, but I was glad to have a name for what had been going on for years.

The doctor only knew that I'd been in this state of mind since

I was 14, which was when I first told someone that my dad sexually abused me. But I'd had some problems with reality since I was a young kid.

When my mom and dad started using drugs, I was crying on the inside while I was calm on the outside. When my dad started to abuse me, I was about 9 years old. My mind went from just imagining basic kid stuff like flying and ice cream to chronic depersonalization. My doctor told me that I felt separate from myself because the abuse overwhelmed my body and mind.

As the years went on, my secret about my dad and about my parents' drug use stayed inside and it caused a deep separation between the world and my mind. So, to this day, when I sit in school or alone at home, I will drift.

The problem with what I like to call "drift" is that, for a while, I couldn't seem to stop separating myself. I'd sit in class and all of a sudden I was outside walking with my dad. Meanwhile my other half was saying, "What are you doing?"

*E*ventually I went into the hospital. I was depressed, hearing voices and cutting myself. I thought that I would be able to work on my problems for two months and get back to high school and graduate. It was my last year.

But I ended up staying in the hospital for about eight months in all, maybe because I cut myself while I was there and acted out. When I got out I was on medication, but I messed with the dose because it made me feel so sleepy. Also, I wanted to believe that I didn't need it anymore.

I ended up back in the hospital. I felt that I needed to go back but I also felt that they were patching up a wound that would never heal.

I was diagnosed with schizophrenia and then bipolar disorder. I was upset. I thought, "Why is this happening to me? Was it something I did? Or was my mother just passing on a family trait that had my name on it?" My mother has bipolar. I believe that she breathed her illness into my lungs when I was a baby and I became an angel held down by its wings.

There were some good parts to being in the hospital. For the first time, I felt like I was part of a family that wouldn't give up on me. The staff helped me realize that I can have an illness or I can be an illness, meaning that I can accept it or it can hold me hostage, taking over my body and mind.

The groups were really hard. I hated when they told me to be assertive. That made me feel like my way of acting wasn't good enough for them and that I had no privacy and had to tell them everything.

During those months in the hospital I missed my prom, my graduation and lost all of my friends. It was like I just watched them move on while I sat in the dark with a cloud over my head.

I took one step forward and my illness took me one step back. My everyday life often felt unbearable and out of control.

I wanted to apologize to my friends for not saying goodbye. I blamed myself and felt ashamed. I felt I was a failure, a freak! When I saw my old friends, they talked to me like this: "Are… you…OK? Did…you…take …your medication?"

Everything about this illness makes me angry. How can I have something inside of me that I don't even want to be part of me? How can I accept being treated like a lab rat trying medication after medication? How can I look in the mirror and see how the meds have changed my face and body and accept that these changes will never go away? Why should I even try?

When I remember my old ways, I think, "That person died." I feel like a person who is broken, lost, and incomplete.

Once I got out of the hospital, I started a new day treatment program in the Bronx. It's not bad. But at first I was hearing voices and having hallucinations a lot of the time. I thought that I was out of the woods, but it was like I took one step forward and my illness took me one step back. My everyday life often felt unbearable and out of control.

"I'm going to the agency for a meeting," Yolanda told me one afternoon.

I got up off the floor. "When will you be back?"

"In an hour or so."

I didn't want to be alone but before I could say so Yolonda said, "I'll be back" and closed the door. Silence. It was peaceful. I was drawing, writing a poem and thinking of my favorite songs. But it was exactly three minutes before something came over me. A voice said, "Do it, why don't you, but don't tell."

I knew what the voice was telling me: it wanted me to cut myself.

I went to my room and picked up the razor. How good it would feel to put it against my skin and cut it. "Do it ...you'll feel better," the voice said. I broke the blade into little pieces. They were shiny and pointy. I'll do it just this once. I picked up a piece, closed my eyes, and pulled it across my wrist. I was listening to the voice. I was feeling scared, frightened and confused.

I knew what the voice was telling me: it wanted me to cut myself.

The blade wasn't sharp. I scraped it along my arm again. Still nothing. Maybe God was sending me a message. I stopped myself, said "No!" and threw it in the trash.

I got up to look in Yolanda's room hoping that she would magically appear, but she was gone. I was alone.

I lay on the floor and cried. I told myself, "You were about to do a stupid thing and you can't blame the voices. You were the one who was crazy enough to listen to them."

I stood at the living room window and waited. Just before 4 p.m. a black cab pulled up. Yolonda stepped out floating like an angel. The voices went away.

I wanted to hug her and tell her to never leave me alone again. But I decided not to tell her anything about what happened. What if she put me in the hospital? I fear that everything

I do or feel will lead me to the hospital.

One of the worst parts of this illness, or the medications that treat it, is that not only have new bad things become part of me, but some of my good parts seem to have left. Yes, it feels good to let go of some of the pain and self-blame from my abusive past. My sad and upsetting parts seem to be inside of me less. But my funny side, the playful way I interacted with my sister, seems to have disappeared, too.

I get so angry sometimes, thinking, "Just a year ago I was a happy young woman with no marks on her face or arms, who felt she could reach for the stars and bring light to the moon, smile just for the hell of it. She didn't have to be ashamed of what she was and what she might become. She was pretty and thin, with nice hair. She cried at sad movies and loved her relationship with her sister."

I know that's not the whole picture. I was drinking, I was afraid at night, I was cutting myself, I was "drifting," I was in pain. But at least I could cry at sad movies and laugh! Now I look in the mirror and see my heavy face, my heavy insides, the scars on my arms. It's too much. Even my thinking is not the same, because of my illness or my meds, I'm not sure which. I feel I'm losing myself.

Often I fear that, because of this illness, I can never dream of finding love. Who's going to want me now? Who wants a woman who has to take medication just so she doesn't freak out?

Sometimes I hate this woman I've become. I don't feel I know her. She takes people's comments without raising her voice when they are hurtful, she cries in the shower, she's fat, she doesn't know what's good for her, and maybe she won't get to be that artist and writer she wants to be. "You're stupid," I say when I see her in the mirror. I would pay a million dollars so I wouldn't have to see her every day.

I am trying to accept the fact that I have a mental illness, but it doesn't seem fair. When I fell apart I thought it was a normal response to my painful past, but then the doctors said that it was also a problem within me, caused by my own brain. I lost my hope of a normal future.

I had already lost my childhood, my innocence, my control over my sexuality and my body, and my family, especially my mother. I felt inadequate, confused, lonely, anxious, uncertain, angry, and burdened.

Right now, I'm doing a little better. I haven't heard voices or seen things in a good two months. That makes me feel I can triumph over this illness. I still can't accept that it might not go away.

Recently I took a trip to Atlantic City with Yolonda, my sister, and my foster family. I did things on that trip that I shouldn't have. I isolated myself and wouldn't leave the hotel room.

But this time, I was also more collected. When everyone was arguing, I didn't jump in, just sat and watched. I felt like I didn't have to be part of something I didn't want to be a part of. I felt proud of myself for that.

I even had fun. I went to the boardwalk, went swimming , took pictures, had a cheese omelet with bacon, and slept in a nice warm bed.

I'm trying to keep up some of the techniques I've learned. I don't yell at my foster sister because she's not my responsibility. I try not to let people or things get me upset, because my reaction is under my power. I separate myself from negative attention. I try to spend time with myself and clear my mind.

In the shower, where others can't hear me, I talk to myself because it makes me feel good. It makes me realize that I have a lot to say. For so long I didn't let myself say things I needed to get out.

Of course, I'm not saying that I'm cured. I'm still on medication. I'm still in treatment. I'm still struggling with wanting to hurt myself. I still find myself lying on the floor, crying. I think the voices and visions will probably come back. My hopelessness is still there, but a little bit of me—the real me—is still there, too. I have the tiniest bit of hope right now that I'm not entirely lost.

The author was 19 when she wrote this story. She aged out of foster care in 2008 and enrolled in college in New York City.

My Guardian Angel

By T. Mahdi

Some people say they have a guardian angel watching over them. I can believe that. I have a guardian angel too. She's my godmother. Her name is Elizabeth. And if there is a God out there, he probably sent her to my sister and me.

I met Elizabeth when I was a little girl. She's the child advocate at my school. She is always taking care of somebody or showing kids right from wrong. She is about my height, with a kind, round face, pretty eyes, caring arms and a voice that shouts, "Put your hat on!" or, "If you don't sit you're on time out!" When I hug her, I get the warmest feeling.

As my home life went from good to bad, my relationship with my godmother grew closer and closer. Each time I had a problem I went to her. I didn't tell her everything, but it seemed that Elizabeth always knew what I was talking about, and each time that I went to her my trust in her grew.

I began to call her at night or I'd visit her when she was at work and I needed someone to talk to. I would say, "Hi, Elizabeth, are you busy?" She'd say, "Hey, gorgeous, how are you?"

Elizabeth is like a mom to me. She's there for me when I need her, like when I'm sad or if I have a bad day. But I also feel confused about Elizabeth, because I have to decide if I want her to adopt my twin sister and me.

My sister tries to push the situation on me by saying, "I wouldn't mind being her daughter, what do you think?" It comes up every six months when the staff gives the girls in my group home a paper asking if we want to be adopted.

My caseworker has a part in it also. She once said, "I would let you guys be adopted by your godmother because she's real nice...and blah blah...she's a sweet person...." I have to agree that Elizabeth is nice, but I'm not sure I want her to adopt me.

Honestly, I want to be Elizabeth's daughter. If she adopted me, I could finally have a mom who I can rely on. I need somebody who would understand me and be there for me and love me like a mom. I don't love my own mom, who put me through so much abuse and pain. I'm glad that I've realized that my mom and I will never be family again, even though it's scary to realize that my dream of reuniting with my mom is over and I finally have to let go.

I still have a lot of pain from my past, and I don't always deal with that pain in the best way.

I want Elizabeth to know that she fills the empty hole in my heart. I'd like to think that if I were her child, I wouldn't be hard to live with. I could do whatever she needs in the house and act like one of her own kids, who are so funny and sweet. I would be nice and respectful to her and her family.

My fear is that if I became her daughter, I would have to get closer to her. I would have to let her see the parts of me that I'm ashamed of, and I'm not sure I'm ready to get that close to anybody.

I still have a lot of pain from my past, and I don't always deal with that pain in the best way. I enjoy drinking every so often. At times I cut myself. What if Elizabeth found out and couldn't handle it?

I think if she knew she would tell me to stop, but it would be scary to stop drinking and cutting, because then I wouldn't have anything to settle me down, keep me calm or cheer me up. What if I couldn't stop? What would she think of me then?

It would be scary to stop drinking and cutting, because then I wouldn't have anything to settle me down.

Now, I'd like to think that Elizabeth will love me no matter what I do, but how much can any person handle? I worry that if she knows me better, she might reject me like my mom did.

Elizabeth's nothing like my mom. She treats me like I'm Taheerah, not whoever she wants me to be, and not like only her mood matters. So I ask myself, "How can I feel like that?" But I'm terrified that if I did something she couldn't handle, she would push me away.

I don't want to express the parts of me that she's never seen before and make her change her mind about me. I don't want to feel like a mistake, which was how I felt at home with my mom. My fear that she'd reject me is so strong that, even though I want us to be close, I can't seem to let my guard down.

I could try hard to hide those parts of myself from her, but I also don't want to change the way I act just to please Elizabeth. I wanted to please my mom so much and tried so hard to be her favorite that I forgot to be myself. I kept my mouth shut about how my father was sexually abusing me, and I pretended that my mother didn't know when she did. I love Elizabeth so much that sometimes I think I would do anything to keep her from getting hurt or feeling sad. That scares me.

Since I've been in foster care, I've been trying to figure out who I am. I do that by paying attention to what feels comfortable to me. If I live with Elizabeth and she expects me to stop doing what's comfortable for me and to pretend to feel things I don't, I think I'll be right back where I started. I'll find out that my fear is true: that I have to act like a person I'm not if I want somebody to love me.

Maybe if Elizabeth did adopt me, I would learn the opposite. Maybe I would be able to tell her, "I need you to let me handle my own problems so I can learn to deal with my problems myself." Maybe she would find out about my drinking and my cutting and tell me what I hope she'd say: "It's OK if that's something that you need to do for yourself right now." Maybe I would realize that I can let her see the parts of myself I keep hidden, and that she won't get angry or push me away.

I want to learn to handle my problems like Elizabeth handles hers. She talks about her problems, and makes jokes about them, and acts like life is going to be OK even if what happens isn't what she expected. I think Elizabeth could help me deal with my past and become the person I want to be—caring and open like her.

But I can't help fearing that whenever something good happens, something bad happens too. When I spoke up about the abuse I went through at home, I thought I'd be moved to a safe place temporarily and that my mother and father would get help with their drug addictions and anger. Well, I came into foster care, but my parents have not gotten help and I'm not part of their family anymore. It hurts to begin to let them go.

Getting adopted sounds like it could be a good thing, but maybe it's safer for me to know Elizabeth as my godmother, because I don't think I can handle that loss if our relationship goes wrong.

The author was 18 when she wrote this story.
She aged out of foster care in 2008 and enrolled
in college in New York City.

Elizabeth Deegan

Living on a Razor's Edge

By P. Carr

When I was about 8 or 9 years old, I began throwing myself down the stairs in school for attention. I'd start off at the top, then just let myself drop, just let myself relax and fall. A few times I broke an arm or a leg, but mostly I just walked away with minor bruises.

The kids in school thought that I was crazy and would laugh at and with me. I was laughing too. But really I thought that they were the dumbest people in the world to stand by and let me hurt myself.

I never thought that they were just kids like me and didn't know any better, because I didn't consider myself a child and I did know better. Common sense told me what I was doing was dumb. My body was telling me too. But something inside told me that people would now have no choice but to pay attention and act on what they saw. I wanted people to see the trouble I was in and help me. But even with my teachers, the help never went further than a kiss and a cuddle.

Home was like a war zone. My mother and I were always fighting over dumb stuff, like how I wore my hair or who ate what. We fought the most over who or what I wrote about in my notebooks. My mother didn't believe that I should have anything that was totally mine. But my notebooks were where I wrote down all my thoughts and feelings, and I wasn't going to let her take that away from me. Often when she didn't like what I wrote, my mother would beat me.

I hoped that every kid went through what I did, the daily beatings, the sexual abuse, the nightmares and just the mistreatment all around. I hoped that what I was going through was normal. Deep down I knew it wasn't.

So around the time I turned 11, I started trying to tell the adults around me what was going on at home. For a long time I wondered when Children's Services would be coming to get me. But no one—not my teachers nor my friends' parents—really seemed to listen to a thing I was telling them.

It's sad to say, but at a certain point, that became OK with me. I still wanted to be saved, but I'd wised up a little, and I no longer believed adults were going to be able to give me the help I needed. Besides, part of me was scared of what that help would mean if it did come. I didn't know if I really wanted to be moved away from my mom and my brothers.

Even so, I kept throwing myself down the stairs. I did it because I wanted someone to hold me and love me. I wanted the kiss and the cuddle. I wanted people to see the pain I was in. I just no longer wanted them to know why.

It was around that same time that my doctor noticed the bangs and bruises and sent me to speak with a counselor. I saw those counselors, off and on, for about two years. They didn't help much. They would ask me questions I couldn't or wouldn't answer, like "why." Why are you doing this? Why won't you tell us why you're doing this? Why won't you let us help you?

I'd already had enough bad experiences with adults, and I didn't believe that these doctors, nurses, social workers and therapists were any different. I could tell by the way their eyes sometimes wandered as I would begin to talk about the abuse at home, or in the way they would cut me off in the middle of a sentence when my session was up.

I wasn't sure I was ready to talk to anyone about what I was doing. But I knew why they couldn't help. They didn't care.

Besides, they were constantly changing, and I was tired of getting a new therapist every other month. I started to believe the saying about things having to get worse before they could get better, because that's the way my life was going.

I stopped throwing myself down the stairs at the age of 12. It didn't seem to be working anymore. I needed something more, something stronger. Something that would numb me to my usual pain and let me feel something new. I didn't know what form that new pain would come in. It took me a year to figure it out, but when I did, there was no turning back.

I picked up the razor and tested the blade by pressing it into the palm of my hand. I was 13 years old and sitting on the edge of the bed. I wasn't thinking about anything other than the task at hand. I just wanted to prove to myself that I had the guts to do it, that I wasn't going to back down.

I don't know how I made up my mind that cutting myself was an option, but when I started, it just felt right.

At home I was dealing with the same pain day in and day out. There were days when the beatings were really bad and I couldn't get away from the pain. Those were the days that I wished, prayed and begged for numbness. Those were the days that I just wanted to crawl up inside of myself and disappear.

On those days, cutting seemed like a way to forget about the pain inside me, a way to feel something bigger than myself.

But other days I couldn't feel anything. No matter how I tried, no matter what I did, cold and empty is all I felt. Then cutting seemed like a way to feel something, anything, again.

And I wanted to do something to me that my mother wasn't already doing. I guess in a way I wanted to have more power over me then she had or would ever have. Once I figured out what I was going to do, the next question in my mind was how and with what.

I didn't think a kitchen knife would do. All the ones in my house were big as hell and I wasn't ready to lose an arm or a leg if I somehow messed up. I couldn't very well ask my mother for money to buy a box of razor blades because she'd want to know what for. Glass was sharp enough, but where would I get it without breaking something? You see, I had already made a conscious decision to keep this to myself. This was going to be something that belonged to only me.

After much thought, I decided to use one of my mom's shaving razors. It wasn't the easiest thing to use, but my mom wouldn't miss one out of *I picked up the razor and tested the blade by pressing it into the palm of my hand.* a pack of 10. First I tried to use it as it was, but I couldn't get the blade close enough to my skin. So I had to break it to get the razor out. It took me almost a whole day to get it ready.

Next came the how. I'd just find where I wanted the cut and apply pressure. But how much pressure? How deep did I want these cuts? How long, how short, how visible did I want them to be?

I put the razor blade on the biggest vein I could find. Did I want to kill myself? No. I wasn't ready to die, of that I was sure. Anyway, if I died, I didn't want it to be in the room I shared with two of my little brothers. I loved them more than anyone in the world, and I knew that they wouldn't understand. So I moved the razor away from my vein to the side of my arm.

I decided to do the first cut quick, to get it out of the way.

That first cut was the worst because it was the first. But the sight of blood was exciting. It made me feel strong. I thought that now I held the power, that control was now mine and I could do with it as I wanted.

I let the blood flow, and I made a promise to myself to stop cutting if it ever got to be too much. I didn't keep my promise. I was stupid.

The day after those first cuts I felt like a wanted criminal. I thought everyone would somehow sense what I had done and I would get beat. No one did.

Soon I did it almost every day, more than once a day, until there wasn't an empty space left on my arms. Then I started on my legs. It became like an addiction, like a drug. I needed to do it. I wouldn't go as far as to say that it felt good, but it did make me feel whole, as if I had just eaten a full meal.

My biggest problem in those days was finding a private place to do it. My house wasn't very big. There were only two bedrooms and there was a lot of us, my three brothers, my mother, her boyfriend and me.

I'd do it after everyone went to bed on the floor of my shared bedroom. I used the light from the bathroom to see. No one seemed to notice my late night activities, or that it was 90 degrees and I was wearing a long-sleeved shirt and jeans. Back then no one cared. That's why nobody had a clue.

It got to the point where all I was worried about was where I was going to get my next razor. It became important to me like nothing else. It was more important than my writing, and back then I didn't know how not to write.

When I started cutting myself, it made me feel strong. But eventually it made me feel more vulnerable than before, because now I was a little girl with a big secret. My secrecy stole away any hope of getting help or getting better.

Finally, my secret was forced from me. When I was about 14 or 15, I was hospitalized—I'm not getting into why. But once I was in the hospital, of course the doctors and nurses saw the cuts on my arms and legs. They asked questions like, "Who did this to you and why?" But those questions didn't faze me at all because they were easy to answer.

"Doctor, I did it to myself."

"Why?"

"Because I wanted to." Telling them that was easier than telling them about the need and the numbness.

In order to be let go, they told me I had to go to therapy twice a week. Once there, my m.o. was the same: Sit there because I have to but don't say a word.

It became like an addiction, like a drug. I needed to do it. I wouldn't say it felt good, but it did make me feel whole.

Over time, I saw that these therapists were different. I guess that they had dealt with kids like me before, so they were willing to wait. Eventually we started to talk—about school, girls, my mom and brothers—and I kept on seeing them after I went into foster care, at age 16. I trusted them more and liked them more than all those other adults before. But I still wouldn't talk about the cutting. I don't today, either. I'm just too used to keeping my pain to myself.

People ask me why I started cutting, why it became so important that I couldn't or wouldn't stop. I don't know how to put into words.

I don't even know if I should describe it, because those feelings feel crazy and dirty. Like I'm some pervert making a little kid do something she's too young to know not to do. Like there's a part of me who's older and in control of the cutting. And then there's the little girl part of me who can't ever protect herself, can't fight back, doesn't have a voice to say, "No."

I still cut myself. It has become a security blanket of sorts, something to calm me down when life's too much, or work me up when the world gets too dull or beyond my understanding. I wish I didn't have to go to such extremes to keep my world level, but right now I do.

But I'll tell you another thing, too. Cutting myself hurts and always did. Telling this story hurts, and I'm really glad it does. In a way, it's like I'm cleansing my soul, telling a secret that I should have told a long time ago.

I'm not writing this story to tell those of you like me to stop. It's not my place. I'm also not writing to tell those who are considering it not to. I'm writing this to let you know that I know how it feels to want to have control over yourself and then somehow lose all control. I believe that there is help out there. I just haven't gotten to the place where I'm ready to find it.

Tha author was 20 when she wrote this story.

YC Art Dept.

Who Cuts and Why

By Christine M.

I interviewed therapist Kate Dunn about why people cut and how they can stop.

Q: What is self abuse and why does it happen?

A: Self abuse is anything that injures a person's own body or mind. Some people find self abuse releases feelings that otherwise they couldn't stand.

Self abuse is more common among people who have been abused before. Often with people who have been abused, there's a dissociative process where what's happening to them is so horrific that they can't emotionally stick around. Their mind separates from their body during the abuse. Over time it gives you a relationship to your body that has a certain distance to it, not as if your body isn't real, but as if it isn't yours. It's easier to hurt yourself if you are detached from your body.

Teens who self-mutilate also often come from families where negative emotions aren't expressed, so they don't know how to express pain or sadness. Cutting may be a way to release those negative, intense emotions when they get unbearable. They may find cutting grounding, as well. It brings them back into their bodies and a sense of self. It makes them feel more real. It turns emotional pain into physical pain. Sometimes when people cut they are drawing a line between what happened before and now.

Q: As a therapist, how do you help someone who abuses herself?

A: The thing about self-mutilation is it does work in the short-term, because it makes the person feel better, so it takes a long time for someone to stop self abusing. But it's absolutely necessary that self-mutilation does stop. It's dangerous.

I believe that when you understand something, you can have mastery over it. So I'm interested in understanding the feelings and thoughts and past relationships that cause a person to self abuse. Learning self soothing techniques is also important to helping someone stop.

Q: How should friends react to an individual's self abuse?

A: A lot of times when someone cuts, they'll tell other people they've done it. People who hear about it may feel helpless, because the self-abuse already happened and it's very frightening. So they may be mad or horrified or feel they've been manipulated.

I think it's really important when someone says they're self abusing to express concern, and let that person know that because you care about them, you can't let them continue doing this. People who self abuse need help, and it's sometimes important for them to be reminded that feelings pass, they don't last forever. They need to learn how to manage horrible feelings by distracting themselves instead of abusing themselves.

Q: What can a self abuser do to help herself?

A: Get help, and find different ways to soothe yourself—exercise, cooking, washing dishes. Many self abusers find meditation helpful because it grounds them. Most people find it difficult to harm their body if they feel attached to it. If you do cut again, you have to consider it a lapse, not a relapse. Just because you have an episode of self abusing once, doesn't mean that you have to keep doing it.

How To Get Help

If you know someone who is a cutter, try to be understanding of the pain they're going through. But know that being their friend does not mean keeping their secret. If a friend has told you about their self-abuse, it means that they want to get help.

If you are a cutter, even if you feel you can't talk to your parent, it's important that you talk to someone. I know I never would have made the first steps toward recovery without having someone to talk to. Look for an adult you trust, or call:

S.A.F.E. (Self-Abuse Finally Ends) at 1-800-DONT-CUT or 1-800-366-8288. www.selfinjury.com

—Christine M.

Michael Cordero

A Long Hard Climb

By Gia M.

They say life is like one giant mountain—you start at the bottom and climb to the top. But some people's mountains seem steeper than others. And as I got older, I started to wonder whether I could climb mine at all.

I wouldn't say I was depressed all my life. For a long time I didn't even know what that meant. But I can say I was never happy.

I was just the quiet little sweet girl who everyone liked, repressing my hurt and carrying on.

When I was young I had friends, but I was also always something of a loner. My grandmother and I fought all the time, and my relationship with my mother was strained. My home life was never great.

At the beginning of 7th grade, I befriended a new kid named

Alana and we became quite close.

Every day she'd come to my house and we would talk about our lives over screwdrivers. Both of us were striving to be something we were not, trying to look sophisticated sipping from matching glasses, pouring the vodka from a pretty decanter, and the orange juice from an antique pitcher. For a few hours we lived like queens.

But by the middle of the year, Alana was having problems at home, and she ended up in a mental hospital. I went into therapy.

I was depressed. School was hard, home was harder, and the only person I could really relate to had been taken away from me. With Alana, I could really be myself. Without her around, my thoughts turned to death, hate and hopelessness.

I would sit on my mother's bed in the living room and watch TV while sniffing rubber cement.

Things went on like that until the middle of 8th grade. The moping around, the dark moods. A number of times I swallowed a hell of a lot of Advils and went to sleep, hoping not to wake up in the morning.

Around this time, my grandmother was diagnosed with cervical cancer. She went in and out of the hospital for a while before we finally took her home to live with us. Our three-room house filled with the pungent odor of death.

Every day I would force myself to go into my grandmother's room and talk to her. Then, back in my own room, I'd ball up and cry.

I didn't know exactly how to feel. I mean, she got drunk and terrorized me when I was growing up. There had been times when I sat up at night wishing it would be her last night. And now she was dying in the next room!

In a weird way, I felt responsible, like someone up there was trying to make me believe the age-old saying, "Be careful what you wish for." Was this all my fault?

Afraid to sniff glue while my grandmother's nurse was

around, I discovered a new way to release my tension—cutting myself. Not trying to die, just cutting myself. I got a disturbing rush that felt so wonderful.

As my life got worse, I cut myself more and then would go lie to my therapist that my problems at home didn't exist.

My grandmother died a little bit before my 8th grade graduation.

The next year I started going to high school and everything seemed fine for a while. My mom and I moved and I had my own backyard for the first time.

But I'd been repressing my hurt for so long that I snapped.

After 14 years of trying to please everyone all the time, I got sick of putting on an act. Even in school I was never really myself. But it was time to be myself, whoever that was.

I was sick of the constant fights with my mom. Sick of hearing teachers lecturing and pounding useless information into my head. Sick of the world.

My home life had become unbearable. Over the next seven months, I spent more time sleeping on the sidewalk than in my bed.

When I would bring myself home, I would rarely stay for more than a few hours. I'd have something to eat, take some money, and call my friends. At the time, I didn't have enough money for food, let alone a pay phone.

Money only meant one thing: a forty. That took the place of rubber cement and self-mutilation. Then I would hit the street again.

Even on the streets I was playing the role of sweet, quiet little girl. I sat back and watched, finding out who to stay away from and who to befriend.

But I still wasn't happy.

This was just another part of the sad blur that was my life. I would walk around with a smile plastered over held-back tears.

Then my mother took me to family court and things started

to change. The courts and the Children's Aid Society decided that I had to go to therapy, enroll in school (I had been kicked out in 9th grade), live with my mother, and follow the rules. I was put on probation for six months. If I didn't shape up, I'd be put in a group home.

Although my behavior improved then, my mental condition did not. In fact, it got worse. When I refused to go to school the following spring, my mother thought, "Not this again."

She came home one day to find me sleeping in bed, and came over to wake me up. Then she saw my face was stained with the trails of dried up tears.

She pulled the covers back to reveal my arm, which looked as though it had been through a lawn mower. I'd had a date with the butcher knife earlier in the day.

I was depressed. School was hard, home was harder, and the only person I could really relate to had been taken away from me.

My mom frantically woke me up and asked me about my arm. I casually replied, "I was upset."

Yes, I was up to my old tricks again, reverting to my favorite way to let out anger and play with life.

Well, my old tricks led me to a stint at the adolescent day program at a hospital. There I managed to complete the 10th grade and start to feel a bit better about myself.

I spent half of my days there in classes where the work was extremely easy and I felt like a genius. The rest of my day I spent in different types of therapy.

We had groups about anger management, medications (I had been sent to a shrink who put me on anti-depressants) and drugs and alcohol. Most everybody there had done his or her share of drugs.

After the hospital, my mom whisked me away to rural Vermont for a few weeks, which did a body good. My mom and I went swimming in a nearby pond, caught crayfish, and went shopping at country stores. Our relationship got a lot better.

Then, after I came back to the city for a few days, I went to a horse farm in Pennsylvania where I worked and rode for two weeks before enrolling at an alternative high school.

That summer, my mom and I also worked very hard at finding me a good therapist. I started seeing a psychotherapist, went for almost 10 months, and made a lot of progress. I really grew, and I came to a lot of realizations about my life.

I stopped being the little quiet girl. I started expressing myself, which is the greatest feeling in the world.

I'm sure I gained a few enemies because of it, but I also got to see who my real friends are—the people who stood by no matter what, who congratulated my efforts, and didn't try to bring me down with them. They're people who, like Alana, are happy to see the real me all the time, not just in spurts.

I finally realized that the most important person in my life is me. I learned that if my friends are doing something I don't want to do, I don't have to do it. You can't please everyone all the time, and no one expects you to.

For years I had let people lead me around by the nose, never speaking up, always eager to please. Then it hit me—I'm no one else's puppet on a string.

In this world there are very few people who will really try to help you when you need it. I always kind of recognized that, but one day that summer, I saw how true it is.

That summer day a friend of mine was killed, and a bunch of people were going to go to the police station to make a report. But in the end, they didn't because they were too busy drinking.

Growing up in this world, you see a lot of things that no person— especially a child—should ever see. Some people become what they see: the old bum in the gutter, the hooker selling herself to support a drug habit or a slew of kids, or both.

They become the person who gets killed outside a bar on a summer night without anyone paying much attention because all his friends are too busy drinking.

But if you can find one moment to look through human eyes, not the desensitized eyes that you have, things become a lot clearer.

Sometimes when that happens, you're able to pick your own butt up and show everyone you can do what they always said you couldn't.

I started seeing a psychotherapist, went for almost 10 months, and made a lot of progress.

Since that summer, I've been able to make huge strides in my life. For the first time since I was 13, I completed a school year. Not only that, but I'm graduating a year early!

My life still isn't perfect. Life never is. But at least now I'm headed up the mountain. And let me tell you, the view is beautiful.

Gia was 17 when she wrote this story. After graduating from high school, she went on to college and graduated in 2002 with a degree in journalism.

YC Art Dept.

Cutting Away the Pain

By Melissa R.

A couple of years ago, I read an article about cutting. At first, I thought the writer was talking about cutting classes or school. After I read the article, I thought, "How can she do this to her body? I could never do that to myself." I was wrong.

I discovered cutting by accident. And what seemed crazy years earlier began to make terrible sense to me.

I had just aborted an unexpected pregnancy. While my boyfriend Michael supported my decision, and said comforting things like, "I'll be here when you need me," he wasn't.

He didn't come with me to my doctor and he was always busy with work, which felt like an excuse not to see me. I wanted to tell him, "I need you now, so where are you?" But I didn't.

Whenever something traumatic happened to me, I usually did what I could to forget my feelings and memories. I tended to bottle up my emotions because I didn't want to deal with them. But this time it wasn't working.

After the abortion it seemed that everything I'd been through in my life was catching up with me. All the bad memories and feelings were replaying themselves in my head: hurt, pain, misery, anger, stress, and depression. I couldn't take the torment anymore. I was tired of being strong and resisting how I really felt.

I tried to explain to my family, friends and Michael how I felt, but they didn't understand. It seemed like whenever I talked to them, they'd roll their eyes, or make up an excuse like they were in a hurry to meet someone. I felt they were annoyed that I couldn't handle my own problems.

I've often felt alone, even when I'm surrounded by my loved ones. This time I felt abandoned.

My release from these feelings happened by accident. I was helping my mom open a box containing her new stereo system.

I was cutting it open with a knife and I nipped my finger. Normally when I got hurt, I'd cry and whine about the pain, even if it was a paper cut. But this time I didn't feel a thing.

I looked at the drop of blood sliding down my finger. I felt all the suffering and anger leaving my body. It gave me a sense of power and it also gave me a high. I had finally learned how to escape from my anguish.

That night I found my mom's boxcutter in her purse. I took it and her lighter. I wanted to sterilize the boxcutter so I wouldn't get any germs in my bloodstream.

I needed a place to cut where people would never notice, just in case it scarred. I decided to cut my arms. Since it was winter and I wore sweaters all the time, no one would notice. I put the blade on the side of my left arm and pulled.

Disappointment. All I saw was a small indentation in my skin. I thought I didn't do it right. I wanted to break the skin and I wanted to bleed. I wanted to feel that release I felt earlier.

I kept cutting my left arm until I saw slashes form. Then I

proceeded to cut my right arm. After 15 minutes, I decided to stop and clean the slashes with peroxide.

While I was cleaning the slashes, I noticed all the little indentations that I had made earlier starting to show. They looked like scratches. I decided that if anyone asked how I got these cuts, I would just make up a story about a friend's cat that didn't like me and attacked me.

That night I lay in bed thinking, "How come I don't feel the pain of these cuts?"

I figured that compared to the emotional and mental pain I was going through, nothing physical could hurt me as much. Cutting actually made me feel better, not worse, even though I was mutilating my arms.

Every day for about a week, I made a couple more cuts on my arms. Some were just little scratches while others were wide slashes. My arms looked horrible.

I knew I had to keep it a secret because deep down I knew cutting was wrong. I knew I was hurting myself, but I didn't care. I wanted a release from my pain.

I never went below my elbow for fear people would see them. I was afraid that if someone found out I was cutting myself, I would be committed to a mental hospital.

During that week, I felt like I was living two lives. In public I was just the average teen, going to school, hanging out with my friends and going home afterwards.

In private, I felt like a freak, cutting and waiting for the drops of blood to feel happy. I wanted to stop, but I couldn't. I felt that I needed to cut myself to keep going.

I knew I wasn't acting like myself. I kept imagining I was being possessed by some demon who got a kick out of having people hurt themselves. I tried to push the demon out, to be strong and fight all these evil thoughts about hurting myself.

But no matter how hard I fought, I always gave in to the cutting. I felt out of control. I thought it was better to cut myself than to possibly lash out at someone close to me.

But I still had drama with my loved ones. The night before Christmas, my mother and I had a huge argument. Later that evening, I started thinking to myself, "No one cares about you. They will only care when you're dead. Take the knife, put it to your wrist and just slash yourself."

I kept wondering if death was a good idea. I pushed up my sleeves and looked at the veins in my arms. I thought about slashing my wrist and it scared me.

I looked at the drop of blood sliding down my finger. I felt all the suffering and anger leaving my body.

I took the boxcutter and moved it six inches away from the main vein in my wrist. I started to cut and I tried to push the boxcutter as much as I could. Several drops of blood appeared but that was all. I didn't cut anything major.

I felt depressed because at that moment I wanted to die and I didn't do it right. I felt powerless and that I was a failure because I couldn't do anything right in my life, not even kill myself. I have no memory of what I did next but I must've fallen asleep soon afterwards.

The next morning I woke up and realized that I had tried to commit suicide. I thought, "What is wrong with me? Why am I acting like this?" I was scared of myself for trying to take my own life.

My secret fixation was starting to get the better of me, and I wanted to tell someone what I had almost done. I just wanted someone to say, "I'm here for you. You don't have to live with this pain."

But I worried that if I told my best friends, they wouldn't understand the pain I was feeling. I was also afraid they'd tell my mom and I'd be committed.

I wrote in my journal about everything that happened, but it wasn't the same. I wanted to speak to a real person. I really wanted to speak to Michael, but we hadn't spoken all week because we'd had a stupid argument. Since we usually talked on the phone at least twice a day, I thought we were broken up, and I was heartsick over it.

That night, Christmas Eve, my best friend Trisha stopped by on her way home from work to say hello, so I asked her to stay. I didn't want to be left alone and I wanted someone to talk to.

I told Trisha about the problems I was having with Michael but I didn't tell her about the cutting.

I know Trisha cares about me but I didn't want her or anyone else to think I was a freak. Also I was afraid she'd lecture me and tell my mother. But she did convince me to call Michael, to find out if we still had a relationship.

I felt like I was living two lives. In public, I was just the average teen. In private, I felt like a freak.

He was so happy to hear from me. He thought I had broken up with him since I didn't call him in a week, and he started to cry.

When I felt how much Michael really cared about me and our relationship, I told Michael about the cutting and my suicide attempt.

He took a deep breath and asked me, "Why are you doing this to yourself?" My only reply was, "I don't know."

After Michael and I talked, I started to feel much better. I wanted to tell Trisha also, but I didn't. I just opened my Christmas gifts quietly.

I showed Trisha a shirt people at my job had bought me, and I tried it on. When I took off my sweatshirt, I saw Trisha's eyes open wide. "What happened to your arms?"

I looked down. I had totally forgotten I was supposed to be hiding the cuts on my arms. "I don't want to talk about it," I said quietly as I put my sweatshirt back on.

After that night, I knew I wasn't going to keep this secret from my mother for long. Someone was going to tell her or I was going to get caught like I had with Trisha.

Sure enough, two days later, I was getting dressed when my mom had a friend over. Once again I forgot I was supposed to be covering my arms and I went out to greet the friend.

They both looked at me and asked me what happened. I told them the story I concocted in the beginning: My friend's cat scratched me.

I knew my mom didn't believe it. From the look in her eyes, I could tell she recognized what I was going through.

Later that night, I met Michael. He grabbed my arm and pushed my sleeve up six inches. "I don't see no cuts," he said as he examined my forearm. I lifted the sleeve higher where the cuts were. "Now do you see it?" I asked.

He looked at my arm, horrified and shocked. From that look alone I thought he was going to break up with me.

Instead he said, "I'll help you get through this." And this time, Michael did come through for me. Over time he talked to me about my problems and calmed me down when I got upset.

Talking to Michael helped me reduce my cutting, but I couldn't stop entirely. After a few months of cutting off and on, my mom confronted me.

"I'm not stupid, Melissa. I can see what you're doing to your body," she said. "Why are you doing this to yourself?"

I told her the truth, that cutting makes me feel better about myself when I'm depressed.

That's when she told me a secret: She was also a cutter. She showed me the scars on her arms, which were in x shapes.

"What made you stop?" I asked her. She told me when she broke up with my father, she didn't feel worthy of any man.

She eventually tried to cut her ring finger off, but when she felt the knife hit the bone in her finger, it shocked her, and she decided to stop cutting for good. I felt closer to her knowing she'd been there too.

My mother sharing her secret made me realize I had to stop. I knew I would need tremendous willpower. With the help of my mother, I found a therapist who was understanding and down to earth. For several months, I stopped completely.

But then I did it again. My mother's boyfriend had yelled at me. I was enraged. At some point, I must've grabbed a knife in the kitchen, snuck it back into my room, and started cutting.

I snapped out of my rage when I was in the middle of making a cut. I put the knife down and realized I still had a serious problem. I'm too quick to feel strong emotions, like anger. I can explode and I don't know what I'm capable of doing.

I still see my therapist every week. She gives me little pointers on how to handle my anger. She recommends hitting a pillow or a punching bag. It works at times, though the thought of punching someone lingers with me.

Thankfully, I haven't cut myself since September and I don't want to. I do get the urge but I find some way to get past it, like playing a video game or taking a hot bath and reflecting on how I could solve my problems without cutting.

These methods may not eliminate my desire to cut completely, but I find new, positive ways to avoid cutting, like wrestling.

Still, I can't forget my bout with self-injury. Every day I look at my arms in the mirror and they look horrible. There are a lot of scars. But I don't want to get rid of them. I want to keep the scars as a reminder of the mistake I made.

Melissa was 19 when she wrote this story.

James Faber

Cutting: A Cry for Help

By Christina G.

So why do people cut themselves?

Cutting can help people who feel emotionally dead to feel alive again. It can be a release, a form of expression, and a cry for help.

Different people cut themselves for different reasons, said Beth Sklar, a social worker at St. Luke's-Roosevelt Hospital in New York City. But the main reason people cut themselves is to relieve what she called "emotional pain."

Cutting can start because of problems at home and often can be set off by intense feelings of frustration and shame. Some cutters want their wounds to be seen. Others don't.

All use "what's around the house-razors, knives, blades, broken glass" to cut themselves, Sklar said. Some also pull their hair out or bang their heads against the wall.

Cutting oneself seems to be very widespread and cuts across both class and gender lines, Sklar said. She has seen it in both males and females, although she said it has been more reported and studied in females.

Most cutters are in their teens or twenties, but people of all ages may cut themselves.

Cutting is a symptom of larger problems, Sklar said. Most cutters are either victims of sexual abuse, severely depressed or people with borderline personality disorder.

The basic elements of borderline personality disorder are unmet emotional needs, loss of control, detachment from feelings and inability to handle stress.

C utters describe a general pattern to how they feel. Cutting usually begins with a release and a "high," along with feelings of being in control. This is followed by a "low," and feelings of guilt and shame.

"Some people cut themselves whenever a stressful incident happens," Sklar said. They do it for a little while when something traumatic, like a death, occurs.

For others, it "becomes like an addiction...[people] cut and feel relief." They feel a chemical high and continue hurting themselves for the feeling.

People come to treatment by different methods. Although some people will tell a therapist that they're cutting themselves, Sklar thinks the best way for therapists to find out is to "ask whether or not they've ever hurt themselves."

Treatment works best if people admit they cut themselves and want a therapist to help them stop. Others may stop without treatment.

But therapists can help patients figure out what sets it off, find other ways to cope and break the cycle. Therapy can help cutters talk about their feelings and get to the root of what started it all.

Introduction

The following stories describe how therapy and therapists work. Therapist Carolyn Glaser briefly describes what teens and therapists can accomplish in therapy, as well as what therapy can't be expected to do. Then teen authors Natasha Santos and P. Carr describe their experiences with therapists, and how the process has helped them deal with difficult issues. While cutting is not always mentioned in these stories, they show the value of using therapy to find positive ways to face difficult emotions.

Therapy: What It's All About

By Carolyn Glaser

In therapy, people have the chance to talk about what's going on in their lives. They also have a chance to discuss what's affected them in the past, as well as how that affects how they're thinking and feeling now.

Therapy is not supposed to make you the happiest person in the world or make you perfect. It's supposed to make you feel good about who you are and help you live your life to your full ability. It's supposed to help you learn to be competent and deal with hardships, because life is hard.

Sometimes people come and they think they're going to feel better immediately, but they usually feel worse before they feel

---

Carolyn Glaser is a therapist at The Door,
a youth center in New York City.

better. That can last a month, or several months, because therapy is digging, and you're often digging up painful stuff.

It's also important to have the right therapist. Just because a therapist is great doesn't mean that's the right therapist for you. Sometimes you just don't click. It's important to be able to say, "I don't like this, it's not working for me." The therapist should be able to see it too and switch you if it's not working.

In therapy, confidentiality is the most important thing. The only time that should be broken is when someone makes a suicide threat or a homicide threat. Other than that, your therapist should be the one person you talk to who's not going to tell anyone your business. If you don't feel safe, it doesn't work.

Kenneth Ng

Why Go to Therapy?

By Natasha Santos

Many of us have been to therapy, whether by choice or by force. We've sat in a chair week after week talking—or not talking—about our problems. However, we often don't really understand the purpose of therapy. We've come up with our own definitions for our therapists: "That crazy lady who asks all the questions," or, "That man who's always in my business."

Many teens want to know how therapy is supposed to work and how a relationship with a therapist can be healing. So I interviewed therapist Carrie King, director of the Children's Psychotherapy Project in Brooklyn, New York, to sort out all of the ideas we have about therapy.

King was short and slim, friendly but with a sharp tongue. She said many kids have been through traumatic experiences and that spending time in a safe place thinking about what has happened to you is important, because traumas can have a lasting impact. Even if years have passed, your mind and body may still be working out an understanding of a traumatic event that happened to you when you were much younger.

Your feelings might come out through harmful behaviors like self-mutilation (hurting yourself) or eating disorders (bulimia, anorexia or binge eating). These are all signs that your mind and body are trying to work out what happened to you.

To protect ourselves from harm, we may shield ourselves from people or situations that we fear. But those walls can also make us feel isolated or misunderstood.

If you were physically or sexually abused, you might never have fully allowed yourself to experience the feelings associated with what happened. Those feelings can come back in ways that may feel strange to you. For instance, some people develop panic attacks (a sudden feeling of intense anxiety, shortness of breath, sweating and trembling), or hypervigilance (an unusually high awareness of surroundings), or dissociation (a feeling of being separate from yourself and away from your body).

"Kids who are molested grow up wondering if they're good," King said. "They ask questions like: 'Is who I am good enough? Am I good enough in relationships? Am I good enough as a friend?'" Her message was clear: although the abuse many of us endured was not our fault, it often leaves us feeling tainted, unworthy, or like we're bad inside.

King said that if you don't come to an understanding of what happened to you in the past, you might put yourself at a greater risk of being abused again. Many times, people who have suffered a trauma seek out experiences that feel similar to those that led to the painful experience. Just as you may replay the trauma in your head, trying to understand what happened or why, you may unconsciously replay the trauma in your life.

King researched factors that affect whether adult women who had been sexually abused in the past were sexually abused again. She found two things: First, because it feels so bad to be abused, some women got depressed and started drinking or doing drugs. "Anyone on drugs or drinking is at a higher risk of being sexually assaulted," King said, because they are not always aware of their surroundings or what's happening to them.

Second, some women feel so badly about themselves because of the abuse that it changes the way they view themselves and their bodies. "They lose an attachment to or respect for their bodies," King said. So when there were danger signs, these women didn't take action to protect their bodies from harm.

With the right person, therapy is a place where you have the freedom and safety to change harmful patterns of thinking or acting, so you don't get hurt again.

"A repetition of the trauma [being abused in a similar way as in the past] shows you there's still something you need to understand about how you think about what happened, or what it means to you, and how you approach your body and your life as a result," she said.

Because of betrayals we've experienced in past relationships, many of us feel unsure about getting into new relationships. To protect ourselves from harm, we may build boundaries and walls inside to shield ourselves from people or situations that we fear may hurt us.

But those walls—like reacting to other people with distrust or hostility—can also make us feel isolated or misunderstood. I asked if it's possible to loosen our boundaries so we can truly become close to others, and how we could go about doing that without making ourselves unsafe.

"You built that boundary because you love yourself and you had the will to survive," King said. "But when the danger is not there anymore, you have to let go of those boundaries." King said you can take certain steps to rethink how you approach others.

The first step is to acknowledge that you built those walls for a reason: you needed to protect yourself from danger.

The second is asking yourself, "Why did I build this?" Looking back at what you didn't have as a child (like protection or consistent love) and figuring out whether you have it now is a lot of work. It means considering your past and seeing how many things in your life have changed, investigating your mind and environment consciously, and seeing how safe you really are now.

The third step is to begin to take the boundary down. That's a huge thing to do because you're making yourself vulnerable and leaving the familiar. Say someone abused you by constantly cutting you down. You might have become hostile and untrusting of people, fearing that they will do the same thing. But once you become aware of this pattern, you decide to try to let go of your hostility and distrust and connect to positive, caring friends and adults. That's a great goal, but scary. You're leaving familiar ways of behaving and trying out new ways of relating to people that you hope will be better. But being more open might lead to getting hurt again.

When taking any risk, it's best to have someone safe to return to for support and to reflect on the feelings that risk-taking raises inside of you. That's where a therapist can be more helpful than a friend or even a mentor. "It's very hard for a friend to help you feel safe enough to take such enormous risks. In most cases, it takes someone who is trained," King said.

King said therapists can often help their clients hear themselves. She gave us an example of a girl who says she wants to settle down, but is constantly going from guy to guy. "I would try to get her to figure out why she's going from guy to guy if she wants to be connected to one person," she said.

A therapist can help you think about your experiences in new ways. "Sometimes you spend so much time in your own head, you lose the creativity of thinking about your problems in a different way. Telling someone else and hearing his or her ideas on your problems can be good," she told me.

Many of us believe that a therapists' main job is to give advice on the day-to-day goings-on in our lives. But King said she is not there to give advice and solve problems. Rather, she's there to observe and notice her clients' behaviors and to pay attention to the larger themes in their lives, such as the main emotions they feel, experiences they seek out, and patterns in their behavior.

She said therapists are trained to see the big picture. "We try to look for what's behind all the details of a story—the rage, or the fear of being left again, or the worry about what's going to become of you. Those are the bigger things, the big umbrella sort of piece behind many of your stories," she said.

We thought therapists must become bored listening to their clients for hours, but King said even boredom can be useful. "When someone is telling a big long boring story, I use it to think, 'What's happening here? Why am I feeling bored'?" Sometimes people go on and on about something unimportant to avoid talking about something real or important, she said. If the therapist points that out, they can at least talk about why the client is avoiding a more important conversation.

Speaking with Dr. King made therapy seem less scary and threatening. She helped me see that with the right person, therapy is a place where you have the freedom and safety to think and talk about painful experiences in your past, and to get help changing harmful patterns of thinking or acting, so you don't get hurt again.

Teodoro Romero

Opening Up: I Found a Therapist I Can Trust

By Natasha Santos

"So what do you think about that?"

"What do you think I think about that?"

"Well, I think that you're avoiding the question."

For months, that was a typical conversation between my therapist and me. Rachel would ask me a question, and I would ask her the question back. I wasn't going to easily give her access into my deepest thoughts. I had been seriously traumatized by B.S. therapists before. If this lady wanted to me to trust her, she would have to work for it!

That's exactly what she did. I hated it when she would ask me seemingly obvious questions like, "How do you feel?" and insist that I answer them. I usually wouldn't at first. I'd give her an annoyed look and a blank-eyed stare and hope that she would let the stupid question drop. She never did.

I decided to go to therapy when I was 16 because my mother had died, I was having trouble in school, and my adopted family wasn't the best at helping me handle my problems. First I went to my school's social worker, who encouraged me to go to a therapist. I went to the intake (first session) with my mom, feeling very wary and uncomfortable. I was on the lookout for fake pity and stereotyping therapists.

From ages 9 to 12 I had gone to court mandated therapy sessions with my foster mother, who spent 30 minutes telling the therapist how big a liar and thief I was, and the remaining 15 minutes lecturing me about how I could be more loveable if I would just change.

"Just try, that's all we're asking, Tasha," Diane would say with a smug smile on her face. Not really listening, I would nod and smile. My therapist wasn't a very big part of the session. It seemed like she was just there to agree with whatever my foster mother said.

At 14 I returned to the same therapist—and finally realized how clueless she was about my real needs. She was all about dealing with my current problems, like what I had done in school that day or if I'd had an argument with my new foster mother. Her advice felt generic and uncaring. "Talk about it with them" was all she would say. I never did and she never asked for any follow-up.

I stopped going to her after several sessions. I didn't say why. I just told everyone that I didn't need therapy. I felt that no one could do me any good. If I needed something I would have to find it someplace else or not at all. If I was feeling sad or upset about something I would go to my older sister, but even that had its limits. I usually ended up in my room crying and sulking until I couldn't pity myself anymore.

Those were very depressing times.

Then my mother died and school troubles followed. About four months after she passed away I began to fail classes. I felt the need to talk, but I didn't have anyone to talk to. My adoptive mother recommended therapy. But I wasn't going to open myself up to that hurt again. Instead I met with the social worker at my high school. When she asked me if I would consider seeing a therapist, I said no.

But after meeting with the social worker a third time (the maximum allowed), I began to consider it. The school social worker listened to me and seemed to care about what I was saying, so maybe her colleagues would be the same way. The school social worker didn't condemn anything I did, but considered—and asked me to consider—the reasons behind my actions and feelings.

So my mom and I went to the intake just to see what it was about. We sat in the waiting room filling out form after form about my personality and what I was there for and my past history in therapy. I was nervous and slightly uncomfortable.

I wasn't talking to anyone. I'd been against this meeting from the start, and I wasn't going to waste my breath trying to save it.

As we sat in the small waiting room, a group of about 20 kids filed out of a corridor and into the street. "You guys have 10 minutes for a smoke break," a woman called to them.

"Maybe this won't be such a bad place after all," I thought with a slight smirk. "What kind of place is so free as to allow teens to take a smoke break?" Unconventional. Good. Conventional therapy hadn't worked for me in the past.

I started seeing Rachel every week. I like Rachel's persistence. She has a calmness about her, which is good in case I ever decide to go completely emotional. One of my biggest fears is that in the midst of dealing with something I'll go all emotional and do something I can't take back. I've told Rachel about my fear, but she doesn't seem too concerned about it.

She wasn't in a rush to get me to the version of myself she thought I should be. Rachel seemed more human to me than any of my shrinks—she liked to talk about clothes, she listened to music and she's even let me borrow a CD or two. Rachel is real in a way none of my other therapists were.

A couple of months into our sessions, Rachel suggested having a session with my adoptive mom. I had been telling her about how my mom and I were having trouble communicating with each other. Rachel felt that we needed a safe place to talk.

I was completely against it because of my past experience with my old foster mom. But she was insistent, so within two weeks I was sitting across from Rachel and next to my mom, feeling dreary and acting as nasty as possible. If they wanted war, they'd get it.

"So Tasha, why are we here today?" Rachel said.

"I don't know, why?" I said, looking at the floor.

"Natasha, if you want us to help you, you're gonna have to communicate with us," Rachel said.

"I don't need this kind of help," I said, reaching for my third piece of chocolate from the candy dish she kept on her bookshelf.

"Why don't you put down the candy and talk to her," my mom said in exasperation.

I wasn't talking to anyone. I'd been against this meeting from the start, and if it was going to go to hell, I sure wasn't going to waste my breath and energy trying to save it. The session proceeded like that until we left.

My mother exited the room stiff and silent. Rachel seemed severely annoyed. I was oddly pleased with myself. Later that night, at home, I apologized with a smirk on my face and my mother knew I was BSing, so she didn't accept it.

In the next session, Rachel wanted to talk about what had happened. I was interested in her analysis. "You have told me in the past," she said, "that you had been hurt when you had your foster mother in the room. And when you were put into that situation again last week you were saying, 'No! I am not going to do this! Other people have hurt me in this way, and I am not letting you in to do the same thing.'"

"Yeah," I thought, "she got it." Maybe I could trust this one after all.

After six months, I began to open up to her more as I realized that everything we did and spoke about was really on my terms. I wasn't consciously aware that a connection was taking place. I noticed that I was talking more and that I wasn't always dreading the sessions, but I would *"Yeah," I thought, "she got it." Maybe I could trust this one after all.* never admit to trusting her as much as I did. I wasn't sure about how safe my feelings were. Hadn't I allowed other people to get close in this way before, only to get hurt?

Now, after two years, I finally feel comfortable enough to start conversations with her and tell her when I don't agree with her without being rude. I feel like she really cares about what I have to say and I value her opinion as well.

I used to begin a session by telling Rachel to ask me a question. If I liked the question I would answer it, and if I didn't like it I would tell her to ask me another one. Sometimes I didn't want to talk about myself, just what was going on around me or in the world. She never pushed me to talk about myself in every session.

After a while I would freely tell her about what had gone on that day. Soon we were having conversations about Diane (my former foster mother) and the state of black people in America.

Now Rachel and I usually discuss how I've been feeling over the week, and how much of that is from my past experiences and how much of it is a feeling that anyone might have in a similar situation. One time I was telling her about a boy I liked and how afraid I was to approach him. I was mortified that he would say something really mean and self-esteem-destroying to me and I would run home crying.

Rachel asked me how much of my fear came from what I knew about that boy, and how much came from my past experiences living with foster parents and "wanting to be loved and accepted but getting rejection," as she put it.

I eventually came to the conclusion that I hadn't really seen or heard anything that should make me so nervous about approaching him. My fear came from my past. Experience had taught me that if I tried to gain acceptance from someone, they would reject me. (I never approached the guy, though. As is the way of crushes, I was over it in another week.)

Learning how my past experience is affecting my present life has made me more aware of what I think and feel, and more aware of what others may be thinking and feeling. I've become more confident knowing there's more than one way to look at any given situation.

It's taken a long time, but we recently started talking about why I had come there in the first place. It's been a slow process. It's not about how much I trust Rachel but how much I feel ready to deal with.

We haven't gotten around to talking about my mother's death (it's still too painful) but we have spoken about the memories I have of her, good and bad. She hasn't pushed the issue, and I appreciate that.

I eventually changed schools and we spoke about what that meant to me in my educational career and life. I had a feeling of failure and terror similar to the one I'd had when I left Diane's house. We spoke about how a part of me felt that it was essentially my fault Diane didn't want me and that's why I had to leave. And how I felt the same way about my school. We decided that sometimes people and places don't click and that it may not be anyone's fault.

The main thing that we are still working on is my adopted family and my place in it. I was adopted when I was 15 and have found it hard to understand my family, which comes from an entirely different culture. Rachel tries to get me to consider who my mom is and how impossible it is to make someone change.

Just last weekend my mom and I were arguing over the rules in the house and how I should be neater and more respectful of her rules. I felt—and still feel—her rules are unfair and odd. I feel like she wants me to behave like an adult but still treats me like a child. We argued for about an hour until she left.

She hasn't really spoken to me in the past five days and I haven't really had anything to say to her. But I got to thinking last night about how she must feel about me and the place she's had to make for me in her life. Perhaps she's worried that I still don't feel a part of the family, and that I'll start going crazy now that I am 18. Perhaps she's worried that if I haven't learned neatness and respect at 18, then when will I learn it?

I've decided to bring all this up with my mom the next time I see her. Before I met Rachel I probably would never have considered looking at things from my mother's point of view. Rachel taught me to try to see things through others' eyes.

It's a good thing I've done it, too, because I'm only allowed to be in the therapy program until I'm 19. Before I leave, I want to be able to deal with things by thinking them through, and understanding people's limitations. I'm working toward that with Rachel. I feel more confident and safe knowing that I've learned how to think and solve my problems myself.

Natasha graduated high school in 2006 and enrolled at the University of New Orleans, studying sociology.

Keeping It Real

By P. Carr

I've been in therapy since I was about 5 years old. "Why that long?" you ask. Well, I have a mental disability called schizo-affective disorder, and from what I'm told I've had it all my life. Basically what it means is that from a young age I've suffered from depression. Sometimes I also hear voices and see things that other people don't see.

Although I saw quite a few therapists from the age of 5 on, it took me nine years to find one who I felt really gave a damn about me, and six years more to find one who had nerve enough to tell me, "Stop the bull. Let's talk about you."

The first was a counselor at a youth center. Her name was Lisa. I saw some other counselors too, but Lisa was the one I loved most.

I considered Lisa a friend more than I considered her a counselor. I could tell her anything. If it was something that I wanted to keep just between us, I'd ask her not to write it down and she wouldn't. I never asked her to keep to herself something she couldn't, like if I was depressed enough to want to hurt myself. When she told one of her supervisors, I knew she had to and I trusted her to do the right thing by me.

I went into the hospital several times from the time I met Lisa till it was time for us to part. Every time I went, she came to visit when she could. She'd bring me things to eat, coloring books. Once she brought me a pair of socks with Winnie the Pooh. She'd even bring me cigarettes although she didn't smoke and didn't like for me to smoke. She did it because she knew that I wanted them and had no way of getting them myself.

My therapist very rarely let me hide, and that's what I had been doing for far too long.

That's what put Lisa above the rest. She stuck by me and really cared if I got better and was OK. With everybody else, it just felt like talk.

Sometimes, though, Lisa was too soft, too sweet. Once in a while I needed for her to crack so I could see that she was real. She never did. It wasn't because she was weak. Lisa had a temper. I could sometimes see it in her eyes when I talked about some of the things I'd gone through in my life. And it wasn't that she didn't care that kept me from really seeing her anger. It was the fact that she was a professional and still young enough to believe in the textbook teachings they give to counselors.

Six years after I met Lisa, I found a therapist who was just as nice but with guts enough to confront me. By the time I ran into Andrea I needed someone to confront me because I'd lost trust again in therapists, so I talked to them about everyone else but me.

Now Andrea let me go on for a while, talking about my

mother and my friends and anyone else who crossed my mind that day, but I guess one day she just got tired of it.

I came into her office one morning just like every other time and sat down for our hour session. Before I could speak, she did. "Good morning, Princess," she said. "We're going to try something new today. You're going to stop the bull and today I want to hear about you."

I laughed, because I knew that she was dead serious and because I knew it was time for me to start to speak. Andrea pushed me. She'd ask me tough questions and would not back down until I answered them. Andrea could curse like a sailor, which kept me laughing, and when she could relate, she did. It helped that she wasn't hiding herself from me like therapists are often trained to do. Sometimes she made me mad on purpose just so I'd have to confront myself. She very rarely let me hide, and that's what I had been doing for far too long.

Therapy hasn't solved my problems, but every time I went I got just a little bit stronger.

Twice a week I saw her and sometimes twice a week was the only time I didn't feel alone. I left her because her boss said I had to join in on some of the other groups they had and I had no desire to. Sometimes I miss her, but before I stopped seeing her she taught me how to depend on myself a little bit more.

Sometimes when you go into therapy you think that whatever problem you entered with you'll leave without, but that's not true. Therapy hasn't and probably won't ever solve my problems, but every time I went and found someone I could trust, I got just a little bit stronger. I didn't trust every therapist I went to see, not at all, but the couple I did trust made a difference. Maybe one day I'll bump into Lisa or Andrea on the street and I can let them know that I'm still struggling, but I'm also doing better, and I'm glad they had a part in that.

The author was 20 when she wrote this story.

Townsend Press

Lost and Found

Darcy Wills winced at the loud rap music coming from her sister's room.

My rhymes were rockin'
MC's were droppin'
People shoutin' and hip-hoppin'
Step to me and you'll be inferior
'Cause I'm your lyrical superior.

Darcy went to Grandma's room. The darkened room smelled of lilac perfume, Grandma's favorite, but since her stroke Grandma did not notice it, or much of anything.

"Bye, Grandma," Darcy whispered from the doorway. "I'm going to school now."

Just then, the music from Jamee's room cut off, and Jamee rushed into the hallway.

The teen characters in the Bluford novels, a fiction series by Townsend Press, struggle with many of the same difficult issues as the writers in this book. Here's the first chapter from *Lost and Found*, by Anne Scraff, the first book in the series. In this novel, high school sophomore Darcy contends with the return of her long-absent father, the troubling behavior of her younger sister Jamee, and the beginning of her first relationship.

"Like she even hears you," Jamee said as she passed Darcy. Just two years younger than Darcy, Jamee was in eighth grade, though she looked older.

"It's still nice to talk to her. Sometimes she understands. You want to pretend she's not here or something?"

"She's not," Jamee said, grabbing her backpack.

"Did you study for your math test?" Darcy asked. Mom was an emergency room nurse who worked rotating shifts. Most of the time, Mom was too tired to pay much attention to the girls' schoolwork. So Darcy tried to keep track of Jamee.

"Mind your own business," Jamee snapped.

"You got two D's on your last report card," Darcy scolded. "You wanna flunk?" Darcy did not want to sound like a nagging parent, but Jamee wasn't doing her best. Maybe she couldn't make A's like Darcy, but she could do better.

Jamee stomped out of the apartment, slamming the door behind her. "Mom's trying to get some rest!" Darcy yelled. "Do you have to be so selfish?" But Jamee was already gone, and the apartment was suddenly quiet.

Darcy loved her sister. Once, they had been good friends. But now all Jamee cared about was her new group of rowdy friends. They leaned on cars outside of school and turned up rap music on their boom boxes until the street seemed to tremble like an earthquake. Jamee had even stopped hanging out with her old friend Alisha Wrobel, something she used to do every weekend.

Darcy went back into the living room, where her mother sat in the recliner sipping coffee. "I'll be home at 2:30, Mom," Darcy said. Mom smiled faintly. She was tired, always tired. And lately she was worried too. The hospital where she worked was cutting staff. It seemed each day fewer people were expected to do more work. It was like trying to climb a mountain that keeps getting taller as you go. Mom was forty-four, but just yesterday she said, "I'm like an old car that's run out of warranty, baby. You know what happens then. Old car is ready for the junk heap. Well, maybe that hospital is gonna tell me one of these days—'Mattie Mae Wills, we don't need you anymore. We can get somebody younger and cheaper.'"

"Mom, you're not old at all," Darcy had said, but they were only words, empty words. They could not erase the dark, weary lines from beneath her mother's eyes.

Darcy headed down the street toward Bluford High School. It was not a terrible neighborhood they lived in; it just was not good. Many front yards were not cared for. Debris—fast food wrappers, plastic bags, old newspapers—blew around and piled against fences and curbs. Darcy hated that. Sometimes she and other kids from school spent Saturday mornings cleaning up, but it seemed a losing battle. Now, as she walked, she tried to focus on small spots of beauty along the way. Mrs. Walker's pink and white roses bobbed proudly in the morning breeze. The Hustons' rock garden was carefully designed around a wooden windmill.

As she neared Bluford, Darcy thought about the science project that her biology teacher, Ms. Reed, was assigning. Darcy was doing hers on tidal pools. She was looking forward to visiting a real tidal pool, taking pictures, and doing research. Today, Ms. Reed would be dividing the students into teams of two. Darcy wanted to be paired with her close friend, Brisana Meeks. They were both excellent students, a cut above most kids at Bluford, Darcy thought.

"Today, we are forming project teams so that each student can gain something valuable from the other," Ms. Reed said as Darcy sat at her desk. Ms. Reed was a tall, stately woman who reminded Darcy of the Statue of Liberty. She would have been a perfect model for the statue if Lady Liberty had been a black woman. She never would have been called pretty, but it was possible she might have been called a handsome woman. "For this assignment, each of you will be working with someone you've never worked with before."

Darcy was worried. If she was not teamed with Brisana,

maybe she would be teamed with some really dumb student who would pull her down. Darcy was a little ashamed of herself for thinking that way. Grandma used to say that all flowers are equal, but different. The simple daisy was just as lovely as the prize rose. But still Darcy did not want to be paired with some weak partner who would lower her grade.

"Darcy Wills will be teamed with Tarah Carson," Ms. Reed announced.

Darcy gasped. Not Tarah! Not that big, chunky girl with the brassy voice who squeezed herself into tight skirts and wore lime green or hot pink satin tops and cheap jewelry. Not Tarah who hung out with Cooper Hodden, that loser who was barely hanging on to his football eligibility. Darcy had heard that Cooper had been left back once or twice and even got his driver's license as a sophomore. Darcy's face felt hot with anger. Why was Ms. Reed doing this?

Hakeem Randall, a handsome, shy boy who sat in the back row, was teamed with the class blabbermouth, LaShawn Appleby. Darcy had a secret crush on Hakeem since freshman year. So far she had only shared this with her diary, never with another living soul.

It was almost as though Ms. Reed was playing some devilish game. Darcy glanced at Tarah, who was smiling broadly. Tarah had an enormous smile, and her teeth contrasted harshly with her dark red lipstick. "Great," Darcy muttered under her breath.

Ms. Reed ord e red the teams to meet so they could begin to plan their projects.

As she sat down by Tarah, Darcy was instantly sickened by a syrupy-sweet odor.

She must have doused herself with cheap perfume this morning , Darcy thought.

"Hey, girl," Tarah said. "Well, don't you look down in the mouth. What's got you lookin' that way?"

It was hard for Darcy to meet new people, especially someone like Tarah, a person Aunt Charlotte would call "low class." These were people who were loud and rude. They drank too much, used drugs, got into fights and ruined the neighborhood. They yelled ugly insults at people, even at their friends. Darcy did not actually know that Tarah did anything like this personally, but she seemed like the type who did.

"I just didn't think you'd be interested in tidal pools," Darcy explained.

Tarah slammed her big hand on the desk, making her gold bracelets jangle like ice cubes in a glass, and laughed. Darcy had never heard a mule bray, but she was sure it made exactly the same sound. Then Tarah leaned close and whispered, "Girl, I don't know a tidal pool from a fool. Ms. Reed stuck us together to mess with our heads, you hear what I'm sayin'?"

"Maybe we could switch to other partners," Darcy said nervously.

A big smile spread slowly over Tarah's face. "Nah, I think I'm gonna enjoy this. You're always sittin' here like a princess collecting your A's. Now you gotta work with a regular person, so you better loosen up, girl!"

Darcy felt as if her teeth were glued to her tongue. She fumbled in her bag for her outline of the project. It all seemed like a horrible joke now. She and Tarah Carson standing knee-deep in the muck of a tidal pool!

"Worms live there, don't they?" Tarah asked, twisting a big gold ring on her chubby finger.

"Yeah, I guess," Darcy replied.

"Big green worms," Tarah continued. "So if you get your feet stuck in the bottom of that old tidal pool, and you can't get out, do the worms crawl up your clothes?"

Darcy ignored the remark. "I'd like for us to go there soon, you know, look around."

"My boyfriend, Cooper, he goes down to the ocean all the time. He can take us. He says he's seen these fiddler crabs. They look like big spiders, and they'll try to bite your toes off. Cooper says so," Tarah said.

"Stop being silly," Darcy shot back. "If you' re not even going to be serious . . . "

"You think you're better than me, don't you?" Tarah suddenly growled.

"I never said—" Darcy blurted.

"You don't have to say it, girl. It's in your eyes. You think I'm a low-life and you're something special. Well, I got more friends than you got fingers and toes together. You got no friends, and everybody laughs at you behind your back. Know what the word on you is? Darcy Wills give you the chills."

Just then, the bell rang, and Darcy was glad for the excuse to turn away from Tarah, to hide the hot tears welling in her eyes. She quickly rushed from the classroom, relieved that school was over. Darcy did not think she could bear to sit through another class just now.

Darcy headed down the long street towards home. She did not like Tarah . Maybe it was wrong, but it was true. Still, Tarah's brutal words hurt. Even stupid, awful people might tell you the truth about yourself. And Darcy did not have any real friends, except for Brisana. Maybe the other kids were mocking her behind her back. Darcy was very slender, not as shapely as many of the other girls. She remembered the time when Cooper Hodden was hanging in front of the deli with his friends, and he yelled as Darcy went by, "Hey, is that really a female there? Sure don't look like it. Looks more like an old broomstick with hair. " His companions laughed rudely, and Darcy had walked a little faster.

A terrible thought clawed at Darcy. Maybe she was the loser, not Tarah. Tarah was always hanging with a bunch of kids, laughing and joking. She would go down the hall to the lockers and greetings would come from everywhere. "Hey, Tarah!" "What's up, Tar?" "See ya at lunch, girl." When Darcy went to the lockers, there was dead silence.

Darcy usually glanced into stores on her way home from school. She enjoyed looking at the trays of chicken feet and pork ears at the little Asian grocery store. Sometimes she would even steal a glance at the diners sitting by the picture window at the Golden Grill Restaurant. But today she stared straight ahead, her shoulders drooping.

If this had happened last year, she would have gone directly to Grandma's house, a block from where Darcy lived. How many times had Darcy and Jamee run to Grandma's, eaten applesauce cookies, drunk cider, and poured out their troubles to Grandma. Somehow, their problems would always dissolve in the warmth of her love and wisdom. But now Grandma was a frail figure in the corner of their apartment, saying little. And what little she did say made less and less sense.

Darcy was usually the first one home. The minute she got there, Mom left for the hospital to take the 3:00 to 11:00 shift in the ER. By the time Mom finished her paperwork at the hospital, she would be lucky to be home again by midnight. After Mom left, Darcy went to Grandma's room to give her the malted nutrition drink that the doctor ordered her to have three times a day.

"Want to drink your chocolate malt, Grandma?" Darcy asked, pulling up a chair beside Grandma's bed.

Grandma was sitting up, and her eyes were open. "No. I'm not hungry," she said listlessly. She always said that.

"You need to drink your malt, Grandma," Darcy insisted, gently putting the straw between the pinched lips.

Grandma sucked the malt slowly. "Grandma, nobody likes me at school," Darcy said. She did not expect any response. But there was a strange comfort in telling Grandma anyway. "Everybody laughs at me. It's because I'm shy and maybe stuck-up, too, I guess. But I don't mean to be. Stuck-up, I mean. Maybe I'm weird. I could be weird, I guess. I could be like Aunt Charlotte . . ." Tears rolled down Darcy's cheeks. Her heart ached with loneliness. There was nobody to talk to anymore, nobody who had time to listen, nobody who understood.

Grandma blinked and pushed the straw away. Her eyes brightened as they did now and then. "You are a wonderful girl. Everybody knows that," Grandma said in an almost normal voice. It happened like that sometimes. It was like being in the middle of a dark storm and having the clouds part, revealing a patch of clear, sunlit blue. For just a few precious minutes, Grandma was bright-eyed and saying normal things.

"Oh, Grandma, I'm so lonely," Darcy cried, pressing her head against Grandma's small shoulder.

"You were such a beautiful baby," Grandma said, stroking her hair." 'That one is going to shine like the morning star.' That's what I told your Mama. 'That child is going to shine like the morning star.' Tell me, Angelcake, is your daddy home yet?"

Darcy straightened. "Not yet." Her heart pounded so hard, she could feel it thumping in her chest. Darcy's father had not been home in five years.

"Well, tell him to see me when he gets home. I want him to buy you that blue dress you liked in the store window. That's for you, Angelcake. Tell him I've got money. My social security came, you know. I have money for the blue dress," Grandma said, her eyes slipping shut.

Just then, Darcy heard the apartment door slam. Jamee had come home. Now she stood in the hall, her hands belligerently on her hips. "Are you talking to Grandma again?" Jamee demanded.

"She was talking like normal," Darcy said. "Sometimes she does. You know she does."

"That is so stupid," Jamee snapped. "She never says anything right anymore. Not anything!" Jamee's voice trembled.

Darcy got up quickly and set down the can of malted milk. She ran to Jamee and put her arms around her sister. "Jamee, I know you're hurting too."

"Oh, don't be stupid," Jamee protested, but Darcy hugged her more tightly, and in a few seconds Jamee was crying. "She was the best thing in this stupid house," Jamee cried. "Why'd she have to go?"

"She didn't go," Darcy said. "Not really."

"She did! She did!" Jamee sobbed. She struggled free of Darcy, ran to her room, and slammed the door. In a minute, Darcy heard the bone-rattling sound of rap music.

Lost and Found, a Bluford Series™ novel, is reprinted with permission from Townsend Press. Copyright © 2002.

Want to read more? This and other *Bluford Series*™ novels and paperbacks can be purchased for $1 each at www.townsendpress.com.

Teens:
How to Get More Out of This Book

Self-help: The teens who wrote the stories in this book did so because they hope that telling their stories will help readers who are facing similar challenges. They want you to know that you are not alone, and that taking specific steps can help you manage or overcome very difficult situations. They've done their best to be clear about the actions that worked for them so you can see if they'll work for you.

Writing: You can also use the book to improve your writing skills. Each teen in this book wrote 5-10 drafts of his or her story before it was published. If you read the stories closely you'll see that the teens work to include a beginning, a middle, and an end, and good scenes, description, dialogue, and anecdotes (little stories). To improve your writing, take a look at how these writers construct their stories. Try some of their techniques in your own writing.

Reading: Finally, you'll notice that we include the first chapter from a Bluford Series novel in this book, alongside the true stories by teens. We hope you'll like it enough to continue reading. The more you read, the more you'll strengthen your reading skills. Teens at Youth Communication like the Bluford novels because they explore themes similar to those in their own stories. Your school may already have the Bluford books. If not, you can order them online for only $1.

Resources on the Web

We will occasionally post Think About It questions on our website, www.youthcomm.org, to accompany stories in this and other Youth Communication books. We try out the questions with teens and post the ones they like best. Many teens report that writing answers to those questions in a journal is very helpful.

How to Use This Book in Staff Training

Staff say that reading these stories gives them greater insight into what teens are thinking and feeling, and new strategies for working with them. You can help the staff you work with by using these stories as case studies.

Select one story to read in the group, and ask staff to identify and discuss the main issue facing the teen. There may be disagreement about this, based on the background and experience of staff. That is fine. One point of the exercise is that teens have complex lives and needs. Adults can probably be more effective if they don't focus too narrowly and can see several dimensions of their clients.

Ask staff: What issues or feelings does the story provoke in them? What kind of help do they think the teen wants? What interventions are likely to be most promising? Least effective? Why? How would you build trust with the teen writer? How have other adults failed the teen, and how might that affect his or her willingness to accept help? What other resources would be helpful to this teen, such as peer support, a mentor, counseling, family therapy, etc.

Resources on the Web

From time to time we will post Think About It questions on our website, www.youthcomm.org, to accompany stories in this and other Youth Communication books. We try out the questions with teens and post the ones that they find most effective. We'll also post lesson for some of the stories. Adults can use the questions and lessons in workshops.

Discussion Guide

Teachers and Staff:
How to Use This Book in Groups

When working with teens individually or in groups, using these stories can help young people face difficult issues in a way that feels safe to them. That's because talking about the issues in the stories usually feels safer to teens than talking about those same issues in their own lives. Addressing issues through the stories allows for some personal distance; they hit close to home, but not too close. Talking about them opens up a safe place for reflection. As teens gain confidence talking about the issues in the stories, they usually become more comfortable talking about those issues in their own lives.

Below are general questions that can help you lead discussions about the stories, which help teens and staff reflect on the issues in their own work and lives. In most cases you can read a story and conduct a discussion in one 45-minute session. Teens are usually happy to read the stories aloud, with each teen reading a paragraph or two. (Allow teens to pass if they don't want to read.) It takes 10-15 minutes to read a story straight through. However, it is often more effective to let workshop participants make comments and discuss the story as you go along. The workshop leader may even want to annotate her copy of the story beforehand with key questions.

If teens read the story ahead of time or silently, it's good to break the ice with a few questions that get everyone on the same page: Who is the main character? How old is she? What happened to her? How did she respond? Etc. Another good starting question is: "What stood out for you in the story?" Go around the room and let each person briefly mention one thing.

Then move on to open-ended questions, which encourage participants to think more deeply about what the writers were feeling, the choices they faced, and they actions they took. There are no right or wrong answers to the open-ended questions. Open-ended questions encourage participants to think about how the themes, emotions and choices in the stories relate to their own lives. Here are some examples of open-ended questions that we have found to be effective. You can use variations of these questions with almost any story in this book.

—What main problem or challenge did the writer face?

—What choices did the teen have in trying to deal with the problem?

—Which way of dealing with the problem was most effective for the teen? Why?

—What strengths, skills, or resources did the teen use to address the challenge?

—If you were in the writer's shoes, what would you have done?

—What could adults have done better to help this young person?

—What have you learned by reading this story that you didn't know before?

—What, if anything, will you do differently after reading this story?

—What surprised you in this story?

—Do you have a different view of this issue, or see a different way of dealing with it, after reading this story? Why or why not?

Credits

The stories in this book appeared in the following
Youth Communication publications:

"My Secret Addiction," by Christina G., *New Youth Connections*, November 1997

"Cutting Myself Seemed Like an Escape," Christine M., *Represent*, January/February 2003

"When Pain Seems a Relief," by Anonymous, *New Youth Connections*, March 2004

"Too Much Independence," by Anonymous, *New Youth Connections*, April 2007

"Drifting Away," by T. Mahdi, *Represent*, May/June 2007

"My Guardian Angel," by T. Mahdi, *Represent*, May/June 2004

"Living on a Razor's Edge," by P. Carr, *Represent*, September/October 2000

"Who Cuts and Why," by Christine M., *New Youth Connections*, March 2004

"A Long Hard Climb," by Gia M., *New Youth Connections*, November 1997

"Cutting Away the Pain," by Melissa R., *New Youth Connections*, January/February 2001

"Cutting: A Cry for Help," by Christina G., *New Youth Connections*, November 1997

"Therapy: What It's All About," by Carolyn Glaser, *Represent*, March/April 2001

"Why Go to Therapy?" by Natasha Santos, *Represent*, July/August 2007

"Opening Up," by Natasha Santos, *Represent*, July/August 2007

"Keeping It Real," by P. Carr, *Represent*, March/April 2001

About
Youth Communication

Youth Communication, founded in 1980, is a nonprofit youth development program located in New York City whose mission is to teach writing, journalism, and leadership skills. The teenagers we train become writers for our websites and books and for two print magazines, *New Youth Connections*, a general-interest youth magazine, and *Represent*, a magazine by and for young people in foster care.

Each year, up to 100 young people participate in Youth Communication's school-year and summer journalism workshops where they work under the direction of full-time professional editors. Most are African American, Latino, or Asian, and many are recent immigrants. The opportunity to reach their peers with accurate portrayals of their lives and important self-help information motivates the young writers to create powerful stories.

Our goal is to run a strong youth development program in which teens produce high quality stories that inform and inspire their peers. Doing so requires us to be sensitive to the complicated lives and emotions of the teen participants while also providing an intellectually rigorous experience. We achieve that goal in the writing/teaching/editing relationship, which is the core of our program.

Our teaching and editorial process begins with discussions

between adult editors and the teen staff. In those meetings, the teens and the editors work together to identify the most important issues in the teens' lives and to figure out how those issues can be turned into stories that will resonate with teen readers.

Once story topics are chosen, students begin the process of crafting their stories. For a personal story, that means revisiting events in one's past to understand their significance for the future. For a commentary, it means developing a logical and persuasive point of view. For a reported story, it means gathering information through research and interviews. Students look inward and outward as they try to make sense of their experiences and the world around them and find the points of intersection between personal and social concerns. That process can take a few weeks or a few months. Stories frequently go through ten or more drafts as students work under the guidance of their editors, the way any professional writer does.

Many of the students who walk through our doors have uneven skills, as a result of poor education, living under extremely stressful conditions, or coming from homes where English is a second language. Yet, to complete their stories, students must successfully perform a wide range of activities, including writing and rewriting, reading, discussion, reflection, research, interviewing, and typing. They must work as members of a team and they must accept individual responsibility. They learn to provide constructive criticism, and to accept it. They engage in explorations of truthfulness, fairness, and accuracy. They meet deadlines. They must develop the audacity to believe that they have something important to say and the humility to recognize that saying it well is not a process of instant gratification. Rather, it usually requires a long, hard struggle through many discussions and much rewriting.

It would be impossible to teach these skills and dispositions as separate, disconnected topics, like grammar, ethics, or assertiveness. However, we find that students make rapid progress when they are learning skills in the context of an inquiry that is personally significant to them and that will benefit their peers.

When teens publish their stories—in *New Youth Connections* and *Represent*, on the web, and in other publications—they reach tens of thousands of teen and adult readers. Teachers, counselors, social workers, and other adults circulate the stories to young people in their classes and out-of-school youth programs. Adults tell us that teens in their programs—including many who are ordinarily resistant to reading—clamor for the stories. Teen readers report that the stories give them information they can't get anywhere else, and inspire them to reflect on their lives and open lines of communication with adults.

Writers usually participate in our program for one semester, though some stay much longer. Years later, many of them report that working here was a turning point in their lives—that it helped them acquire the confidence and skills that they needed for success in college and careers. Scores of our graduates have overcome tremendous obstacles to become journalists, writers, and novelists. They include National Book Award finalist Edwidge Danticat, novelist Ernesto Quinonez, writer Veronica Chambers and *New York Times* reporter Rachel Swarns. Hundreds more are working in law, business, and other careers. Many are teachers, principals, and youth workers, and several have started nonprofit youth programs themselves and work as mentors—helping another generation of young people develop their skills and find their voices.

Youth Communication is a nonprofit educational corporation. Contributions are gratefully accepted and are tax deductible to the fullest extent of the law.

To make a contribution, or for information about our publications and programs, including our catalog of over 100 books and curricula for hard-to-reach teens, see www.youthcomm.org

About The Editors

Al Desetta has been an editor of Youth Communication's two teen magazines, *Foster Care Youth United* (now known as *Represent*) and *New Youth Connections.* He was also an instructor in Youth Communication's juvenile prison writing program. In 1991, he became the organization's first director of teacher development, working with high school teachers to help them produce better writers and student publications.

Prior to working at Youth Communication, Desetta directed environmental education projects in New York City public high schools and worked as a reporter.

He has a master's degree in English literature from City College of the City University of New York and a bachelor's degree from the State University of New York at Binghamton, and he was a Revson Fellow at Columbia University for the 1990-91 academic year.

He is the editor of many books, including several other Youth Communication anthologies: *The Heart Knows Something Different: Teenage Voices from the Foster Care System, The Struggle to Be Strong,* and *The Courage to Be Yourself.* He is currently a freelance editor.

Keith Hefner co-founded Youth Communication in 1980 and has directed it ever since. He is the recipient of the Luther P. Jackson Education Award from the New York Association of Black Journalists and a MacArthur Fellowship. He was also a Revson Fellow at Columbia University.

Laura Longhine is the editorial director at Youth Communication. She edited *Represent*, Youth Communication's magazine by and for youth in foster care, for three years, and has written for a variety of publications. She has a BA in English from Tufts University and an MS in Journalism from Columbia University.

More Helpful Books
From Youth Comunication

 *The Struggle to Be Strong: True Stories by Teens About Overcoming Tough Times.* Foreword by Veronica Chambers. Help young people identify and build on their own strengths with 30 personal stories about resiliency. (Free Spirit)

Fighting the Monster: Teens Write About Confronting Emotional Challenges and Getting Help. Introduction by Dr. Francine Cournos. Teens write about their struggle to achieve emotional well-being. Topics include: Cutting, depression, bereavement, substance abuse, and more. (Youth Communication)

 *Depression, Anger, Sadness: Teens Write About Facing Difficult Emotions.* Give teens the confidence they need to seek help when they need it. These teens write candidly about difficult emotional problems—such as depression, cutting, and domestic violence—and how they have tried to help themselves. (Youth Communication)

Enjoy the Moment: Teens Write About Dealing With Stress. Help decrease the levels of stress and conflict in your teens' lives. These young writers describe how they cope with stress, using methods including meditation, journal writing, and exercise. (Youth Communication)

 The Fury Inside: Teens Write About Anger. Help teens manage their anger. These writers tell how they got better control of their emotions and sought the support of others. (Youth Communication)

Analyze This: Teens Write About Therapy. Get insight into how therapy looks from a teen's perspective and help teens find the services they need. Teens in foster care write about their experiences with therapy. Some are happy with the help, while others are dissatisfied or confused. (Youth Communication)

Haunted By My Past: Teens Write About Surviving Sexual Abuse. Help teens feel less alone and more hopeful about overcoming the trauma of sexual abuse. This collection includes first-person accounts by male and female survivors grappling with fear, shame, and guilt. (Youth Communication)

Putting the Pieces Together Again: Teens Write About Surviving Rape. These stories show how teens have coped with the nightmare experience of rape and taken steps toward recovery. (Youth Communication)

Sticks and Stones: Teens Write About Bullying. Shed light on bullying, as told from the perspectives of the perpetrator, the victim, and the witness. These stories show why bullying occurs, the harm it causes, and how it might be prevented. (Youth Communication)

Out With It: Gay and Straight Teens Write About Homosexuality. Break stereotypes and provide support with this unflinching look at gay life from a teen's perspective. With a focus on urban youth, this book also includes several heterosexual teens' transformative experiences with gay peers. (Youth Communication)

To order these and other books, go to:
www.youthcomm.org
or call 212-279-0708 x115

LaVergne, TN USA
14 September 2010
196952LV00005B/7/P